Fox Russell

Cross Country Reminiscences

Fox Russell

Cross Country Reminiscences

ISBN/EAN: 9783337256432

Printed in Europe, USA, Canada, Australia, Japan

Cover: Foto ©Andreas Hilbeck / pixelio.de

More available books at **www.hansebooks.com**

BY

FOX RUSSELL

London
REMINGTON AND CO PUBLISHERS
HENRIETTA STREET COVENT GARDEN

1887
[*All Rights Reserved*]

THIS VOLUME IS, BY PERMISSION,

DEDICATED TO

HIS GRACE THE DUKE OF BEAUFORT, K.G.,

BEST OF CROSS-COUNTRY RIDERS

AND

BRITISH SPORTSMEN,

BY HIS OBLIGED AND GRATEFUL SERVANT,

THE AUTHOR.

CONTENTS.

CHAP.		PAGE
I.	Introduction	1
II.	With Foxhounds	19
III.	With Staghounds	43
IV.	With Draghounds	57
V.	With Harriers	78
VI.	Steeplechasing and Hurdle Racing	86
VII.	Conditioning and Schooling	126
VIII.	The Show Yard in relation to Hunters	153
IX.	Crossing a Country	166
X.	Ladies in the Field	187
XI.	Steeplechase Courses and Point-to-Point Races	195
XII.	The Mudbury Hunt Dinner	205

CHAPTER I.

INTRODUCTION.

PLEASANT it is for a man whose hand has oftener grasped a hunting crop than a pen, to sit down and try to put a few notes on paper, of some of the good things he has had the luck to participate in, and indulge in some homely-printed chat—to coin an expression—of good horses and good men. It is, perhaps, the next best thing to "fighting one's battles o'er again" over the walnuts and wine; and what more delightful thing is there than that same talk

— after a rattling burst over a good country — when, with a bottle of the '47 and the prospective cigar, a bright, cheery log fire, and a genial spirit, who has shared your day's pleasures and pains, you chat over your own luck, and your friends' misfortunes?—the latter, I am grieved to say, affording considerably more satisfaction to us than we should care to acknowledge in so many words.

Long may the day be distant when Englishmen shall cease to reckon the subject of such chat amongst their pleasures!

I have often wondered which man gets the keenest enjoyment out of hunting: he who makes it the business of his life, and goes out regularly four or five days a week, or the busy toiler in big cities, snatching his chance day here and there, stopped, it may be, by a telegram, as he buckles on his second spur, and dragged unwillingly up to his office by a change of markets, or to his chambers by an unexpected Brief. One would naturally think the latter was the keener of the pair; but the closest observation has left me still in doubt. A good sportsman is never anything *but* keen, and in discussing this question, one is always reminded of the octogenarian who had been a four-days-a-week man all his life: on his death-bed he said he had but one regret—that he had not smoked less and hunted more! It is certainly just one of those good things in life, that one can never have too much of.

In the way of comfort, I venture to think that between hunting from home, and hunting from a distance, there can be no comparison, and no man would take the latter as a pure matter of choice. In fact so patent is it, upon a moment's reflection, that it would be absurd to dilate upon the difference between hurriedly resigning the good beast, who has carried you all day, to a hireling, without the opportunity of knowing whether he is well "done" or not; bolting into a stuffy, draughty railway carriage, in which, hungry, sleepy, and mud-stained, you are rushed up to town, and perhaps transferred to a still more unpleasant conveyance in the shape of a cab, which eventually lands you at home at so late an hour, that appetite is gone, and a natural disinclination for the bother of " changing " induces you to crawl miserably up to bed without delay. Then again, unless you are a naturally—or, shall we say, an *un*naturally—early riser, recall, oh my reader, the horror you went through at being called at 6.30 a.m., fighting your way dismally into that forbidding-looking "tub" in the grey light, and how the first spongeful of its contents wrung from your agonized body a deafening screech that would shame a Sioux Indian; then the candle-illuminated chin-chopping, called, by courtesy, a shave; the hurried and unsatisfying breakfast, and the final scurry for the train! " Enough to make a man sit up and have his breakfast over-night," as a friend once said to me. I agree with him; but I am afraid the coffee and rolls would *not,* at that unaccustomed hour! I am of opinion that that "breakfast" would have been, for the most part, taken out of a tall tumbler and accompanied by sundry strong cigars—*not* the best way in the world to keep one's nerves steady for the following day's work. No! compare this with the leisurely morning muffin and newspaper, and the quiet jog on to covert afterwards; the comfort of being able to personally superintend your horse's dressing and feeding, and then attending at once to your own, after the day's work is done. No, there is no doubt which we should *choose!* But then we don't all get our choice in this life, and having been myself, for several seasons, accustomed to go off to different countries to report the doings of various packs for the London Press, I speak feelingly on the subject!

Whilst speaking of hunting, away from home, I may say, thankfully, that I have very rarely been guilty of the weakness of taking a horse of my own. Hiring is far and away the better plan. First, because you are spared the intolerable nuisance of boxing and unboxing, the danger of a horse, stiff and tired, standing still for hours, in the most favourable circumstances for catching cold, a matter in which he will be sure to attain a certain measure of success; secondly, because it is long odds he will not know the country when he gets there; thirdly, because it is generally cheaper in the end.

I don't know whether the experience of most men coincides with my own, or if I have been exceptionally fortunate, but, taking them all round, I have very pleasant memories of hired hunters. One youngster —a four-year-old, by King of Trumps— I well remember fairly raced his field to a standstill at the end of a long run, with my 8st. 7lbs. on his back; another carried me gallantly throughout one of the fastest hour-and-a-half's runs that the Blackmoor Vale have had for many a season, and finished in the first four. I could multiply such instances by the dozen, and it is comparatively rarely that one of this much-abused class has put me down. Of course it may well be that my phenomenally light weight has something to do with it, but still there is a great deal of good in them, and a wise owner will always, for his own sake, do well to give you a "performer," because, of course, should he fall, and harm come to him, he alone has to pay the piper. To all who are obliged to hunt away from home, I would certainly say, "Don't take your own horse, if you can manage to hire;" and do we not all go a bit straighter (especially in a strange country) when we feel that it will make no difference to the exchequer if "grief" should, by chance, result?

If a man has a week or two to spare from business, and wants to get as much sport into the time as he conveniently can, I would certainly recommend him to go to a place like Leamington, for instance. From here, the Quorn, the Pytchley, the Heythrop, the Bicester, the Duke of Grafton's, the Warwickshire, and the Atherstone packs can all be reached;

so one need never want for a gallop. In addition to its hunting attractions there is generally plenty to keep one amused there, and it is within comparatively easy reach of town. Cheltenham is another handy centre, but the country is not so good as that get-at-able from the Warwickshire town. I say "get-at-able," and not "immediately surrounding," because, as a matter of fact, the country just outside Leamington is not, by any means, the best obtainable.

Hunting on the foregoing plan, the advantage of hiring becomes at once manifest. Assuming you are at any convenient centre for hunting, and want to get in, say, five days in the week you are there, that would mean at least three horses; and by the time you had paid for their railway expenses, standing at livery, and your groom's bill, you would probably find that, had you hired, you would have been considerably in pocket; your own horses would have had a rest, instead of being hard-worked and harassed by railway journeys and fresh stabling, and you yourself would have been spared a very great deal of anxiety and bother about them. I am quite prepared to admit, however, that if one is no longer young, or if one's nerves are not as they used to be, &c., the matter is a different one; and it may well be that the extra expense is worth incurring, for the sake of being on horses that one knows. "Nerves" have a long list of sins to answer for: how many falls might yearly be averted but for the possession of these undesirable adjuncts to the human frame! How many a horse is pulled into his jumps because of the slight shake of the rider's hand, or the quiver of his body! Whilst denying the danger of

INTRODUCTION.

riding to hounds, *in toto*, would be ridiculous, yet I do venture to say that that danger is not really so great as people generally think. Look at the total number of men who hunt; then take into consideration the large proportion of "duffers" amongst them, and it is really surprising how few deaths are heard of, nay, how few bad accidents occur, in each season. And, again, there are very many men who "know how to fall," and show an astonishing smartness in getting out of the way of their own, and other people's, horses, whilst on all fours! Dick Christian was a notable example of this—quite a professor, indeed, of the art. He used to say that he tucked his head in and rounded his shoulders when he "knew it was coming;" but I don't think it is an art that can come to any of us, except by means of the bitter school of experience. Unlike our friend Ally Sloper's advice to people about to be kicked, to "take it slack," we cannot either do this, or reduce falling to a science, and lay down rules thereon. Personally, I have had my fair share of falls, have been laid on by a steeplechase horse, kicked on the head, my ribs broken, and a few other little matters of the kind, but never *really* hurt. The human carcase is fairly tough, I fancy; and though not a particularly strong man, I remember getting two rattling falls in one run, receiving a pretty smart kick just over the knee, and then riding home in time to go to a ball and dance until four o'clock the next morning! The fall itself so rarely hurts anybody; it is the injury inflicted by the horse, either in rising, rolling over you, or kicking you, that is most to be feared. Again, there is the risk of being jumped on, or galloped over, by other animals; and nine out of ten of the bad accidents, happen in one of these ways.

On the subject of wire fencing I must say a word. Some men have now put up *barbed* wire, and on this point the Hon. Ralph Nevill, Master of the West Kent Foxhounds, has written an eloquent letter to the papers, telling how his hounds have been injured by this cruel contrivance. Surely such things should find no place in a hunting country. Wire is bad enough, and has been the cause of many a valuable life being sacrificed; but to put in barbs is both unnecessary and cruel. I can't help thinking that it would be—well, not an impossible task, for each hunt to come to some arrangement with the farmers within its precincts, for the removal of wire-fencing, except in such parts as horses and hounds are not likely to penetrate. Members of the several hunts would willingly make some pecuniary sacrifices for such a desirable object—after all, it is only paying a small extra premium by way of life assurance!—and the main body of the farmers have got sportsmen's hearts concealed within them, though some *have* hidden them rather deep beneath their waistcoats! The truth is that they have had bad times for many years, and wire-fencing being cheap, they very naturally use it. Still, in so doing I know that, with many of them at all events, good fellows at bottom, they can say with the apothecary in *Romeo and Juliet,* " My poverty, but not my will, consents."

To men who must, perforce, hunt from London, I would say, " Don't be afraid of going a few extra miles for the sake of a better country." Practically it takes you out of bed, very little, if any, earlier than travelling down to the countries nearest to town; not that there is a word to be said against the packs there in any one respect, be it understood. It is merely of the country, to which a cruel fate has relegated them, that I speak, for, what with a trot—often you can't shake your horse up to go any faster than this—over the cruel, holding clay, a crawl up hills like the side of a house, and a spirited burst over fifty acres of flint stones, ending the performance by falling over a wire-fence into a market-gardener's cucumber frame, and you are reluctantly obliged to own that the game is hardly worth the candle. I am speaking more particularly of the nearer suburban meets.

Some of the fixtures of the West Kent, near the Kennels at Otford, or round Penshurst way, are as good as anything that can be expected so near London; and the Surrey Stag, and Old Surrey Foxhounds have each some very good meets.

The Mid-Kent Staghounds, having their head-quarters at Wateringbury, near Maidstone, run over a far better line of country than any of the above-named packs, and are infinitely to be preferred by the metropolitan contingent; another recommendation is that they do not meet till twelve o'clock. The Crawley and Horsham Foxhounds can also be reached fairly easily, and with these last two packs I have had some really good spins. The Warnham Staghounds go, three days a fortnight, over the same country as the Crawley and Horsham.

In Essex, the farmers don't seem to take kindly to pasture, and the amount of heavy plough there is not inviting. Mr. Garth's hounds are handy, but I regret that, never having had the pleasure of meeting them, I can say nothing of the sport usually obtained. To my mind, nothing so well repays the Londoner for his trouble, as hiring from Leighton, or Aylesbury, and going for a spin with Lord Rothschild's splendid staghounds over the glorious Vale of Aylesbury. What a country! Grass, grass, and splendid grass too! so springy that your horse seems to strike it lighter and bound from it quicker, than any other. Then the fences —are they not positively made to be galloped over! All of them fair, most of them big, and not one trap in a hundred of them! Yes, that is the country for the brain-worker to go to and "knock the stuffing out" of his cares and troubles! The deer are straight runners, the pack and the whole establishment undeniable, the country perfection, and the farmers, trumps to a man! A good mount, a fine day, and a fast fifty minutes over the Vale, *ought* to make a man of one, if anything can on earth!

Apropos of a fast fifty minutes I was riding home after hunting, some two or three years back, with half-a-dozen other men; we were all in capital spirits, having had a fifty minutes on the grass, with "fencing to match," that was calculated to gladden the heart of an undertaker, when the following conversation ensued:—

"What's become of Jones, of the —th? Never seems to come out at all now."

"No," was the reply; "sold off his horses, don't you know."

"What on earth for?"

"What! haven't you heard? Going to be married next week."

"Married, and sold off his horses!" came in tones of intense disgust from the first speaker. *"Why, I wouldn't have missed to-day's gallop for a harem!"*

CHAPTER II.

WITH FOXHOUNDS.

FOXHOUNDS seem to assume the premier place, naturally, in the affections of most hunting men—that is, with men who go out to *hunt,* in contradistinction to the men who go out to *ride.* For the latter class, by far the best fun is to be had with stag or drag hounds, of which more hereafter. But he who wishes to follow the " little red rover " will, I think, have far better *sport* than the others, modified, of course, by here and there a blank day, here and there an unsatisfactory run. These are exigencies we must all be prepared for. Now, as in everything else, there are degrees in foxhunting: there is foxhunting and foxhunting; galloping over flints, clay, and boulders is one thing, galloping over soft, springy turf another; scrambling over impossible stone walls one thing, and jumping clean timber another. It *has* fallen to my lot to hunt in a country where, with heaps of foxes, we never got a run, except for about the space of three minutes at a time, which was occupied in rushing our quarry from one big wood to the next big wood. We usually got one of these "runs" each day we were out, and spent the rest of the time in mournfully wandering round and round the covert in which Reynard was, no doubt, safely ensconced, and chuckling at his own smartness; then we heaved sighs, and departed severally to our respective domiciles. Well, it *was* foxhunting; but it might as well have been needle-hunting in the proverbial haystack, for all the sport we had out of it.

Coming home after one of these depressing days, a disconsolate companion once said to me, desperately —

"I shall give this up, and invite all the men I know to a meet at the foot of my stairs, and hunt blackbeetles in the back kitchen; *we've a better chance of a kill there, anyhow!*" To this he added some painfully wrought-up joke about "kitchen a lot of them," which I must decline to repeat *in extenso*.

Compare this kind of thing to a glorious burst over the grass, with really good fencing, and there you see the two extremes. But between these Poles there is a big range of ground, containing much that is pleasant—much that will afford excellent sport both for young and old.

Such writers as Whyte Melville and the joint authors of the "Badminton Library" have written of the "swell" countries so well, and so exhaustively, that I feel it would be more useful for me not to attempt to follow where they have "gone before," but to confine myself rather to those others that they have not dealt, or have but superficially dealt, with, in their respective works on the subject.

I venture to think that there is just as much good fun to be had outside Leicestershire as there is in. Look, for instance, at the Blackmoor Vale Foxhounds. Who can reasonably wish for anything better than to follow this splendid pack from Jack White's Gibbet, or Cheriton, right across the huge pastures, interspersed with the big doubles and brooks, for which this district is famed. You must have one that will face water and jump *boldly* at everything here, or you had better go back at once; it is cheaper in the end. Or, nearer home, if you cast in your lot with anything going across the Vale of Aylesbury, and "happen on," as our American friends would say, a good thing, you must be hard to please if you don't go back satisfied, invigorated, and feeling enabled to "make things hot" for everybody in business next day.

One more example : take the Crawley and Horsham Foxhounds. *All* their country is not good ; a large proportion is, perhaps, only passable, but I, for one, shall look back to some of the runs I have had with them, and some of the country I have crossed after them, with the keenest pleasure to the end of my life, despite the contemptuous and, I must add, silly remark of a distinguished soldier, who, when asked if he had ever been out with these hounds, blurted out, "No, sir; I have never hunted with any hounds in my life but the Quorn and the Pytchley, and I'll take d—d good care I never do!" chronicled by Whyte Melville, who, I am sure, was far too good a sportsman to have subscribed to an observation half so absurd.

It is not given to everyone to hunt in the Shires, but it is given to a good many (with an effort) to hunt somewhere or other, either in their own neighbourhood, or within reach of London, and, as the inimitable Jorrocks observes, "the iron horse is the best kiver 'ack in the world."

What would our forefathers have thought, I wonder, of a man working hard at his business overnight, rising with the—we had better say sparrow—there are no larks in London, at least not from the ornithologist's point of view!—travelling fifty or sixty miles to the scene of his day's hunting, enjoying that, and returning the same night to dine at eight, in the neighbourhood of Hyde Park? And yet how many do so, year after year.

You may, however, get plenty of sport, even from London, without having to work for it quite so hard as this; and by taking a pack, say about thirty to forty miles from the great metropolis, you can get into a decent country, and yet not have to do any violence to your feelings in the way of early-rising. Indeed, I knew of a "counsel, learned in the law," who appeared before the late Vice-Chancellor Malins—himself a lover of the horse, but a terribly bad man on one!—in leathers, boots, and spurs, which were barely hidden by his gown, and who made an application at the sitting of the Court, and was even then in time to catch his train and turn up punctually at the meet!

"What a cruel thing foxhunting is!"

exclaimed a lady of my acquaintance, who is nothing if not humanitarian.

"Who to? the hounds or the horses?" queried the man she addressed, and I think there is a good deal of truth in his remark.

If a good fox gets away with that fair start which is, or ought to be, the ambition of every man in the field to give him, I think he has a bit the best of the deal, and, bar accidents, will make both hounds and horses sob, before he is beaten himself.

And bear in mind, too, that when he *is* beaten, for absolute running, the end may be still a remote contingency, for a fox is as full of tricks as an egg is of meat (this may not be an exactly happy metaphor, as I have never yet found either beef or mutton in an egg. I have chicken, though!) First of all, he can swim like a duck, run like a race-horse for a mile, climb a tree, or crawl through a key-hole—if it is large enough! Add to this that he is perfectly *au courant* with the mysteries of scent, and a master of the art of destroying it, is a perfect perambulating atlas of the surrounding country, and is as game as a pebble, and we see at once that hounds have their work cut out to successfully compete with Nature's smartest production. You will always notice that a fox's first instinct is to get out of sight, and it is fairly astonishing to see how cleverly he effects this, even in the most open country. His next move seems to be to determine, in his own mind, the particular point he will make for; he will remember the existence of a friendly earth, perhaps some five miles off, and for that he goes. Watch how he lays himself down to his work, looking back over his shoulder, now and then, at his pursuers, until he has, at least, deprived them of the pleasure of hunting him by sight; then, taking advantage of anything that may turn up to aid him in foiling the scent, onward he goes, disdaining to sneak up hedgerows, or lie in ditches, until the pace begins to tell upon him; then it is that he no longer feels himself equal to taking the straight line across the open, but looks about him to see where he may find a temporary haven in which to recruit his failing strength. Finding none, he again resolutely faces his task, the hounds, by superior staying powers, slowly but surely gaining on him. A park paling looms in sight, and Reynard is quick to take advantage of it. Running along the top, he seems to chuckle at the thought of even temporarily bothering his pursuers. Gaining three or four minutes by this ruse, he scrambles onwards, his back now arched and brush almost dragging on the earth as he goes. At last he sees the little fir patch, concealed within which is the longed-for hiding place. Hounds are now within a hundred yards of him, and throwing tongue in sounds that convey news of joy to all the field within hail, and death to the quarry, unless he can make good his point. They come nearer and nearer, but plainer and plainer gets the belt of firs; now the leading hound, straining every nerve, overhauls him, stride by stride, until she gets to within twenty yards of his brush. Foxey looks sharply over his shoulder, and then, distressed as he is by the severity of the pace, seems to coolly calculate his chances. Only a space of a hundred yards or so remains to be traversed. Melody does all she knows to lessen the gap between them; she is closely followed by another old hand, Madrigal; they are metaphorically licking their chaps over the anticipated " blood," they get closer and closer to his brush, it is almost within reach, they have him! No! with one ugly snap round, he dives like an eel into the unstopped earth and is safe!

"Capital spin, as near as possible half-an-hour. No good trying to dig him here, you know," are some of the remarks made, as the first flight come up, by twos and threes.

No, my friend, it's no *good* digging him, under most circumstances; to my mind it always savours too much of butchery, and taking a dirty advantage, this same digging. He has given you a good run; what more did you come out for? For my part if I *only* wanted to see an animal *killed*, I could have achieved my object by going to a slaughter-house.

"But the hounds want blood; they have deserved it," cry a chorus of sportsmen.

Well, in this world, we all want a great

many things, but we don't get them; we all, at least in our own estimation, *deserve* a good many things, but we don't get them for all that. As to the plea that hounds lose their keenness by being occasionally deprived of their reward, I simply don't believe it. Depend on it, they will be just as fond of the game next time they run. Then, again, you can hug yourself with this, that a fox who has given you one good run may very likely afford you another upon some subsequent occasion. Leave him now, eat your sandwich and take a pull at the flask; trot off to draw for a fresh fox, or, if it is too late, light your Laranaga and jog quietly home, thinking to yourself that there's nothing *quite* so good as foxhunting after all, and mentally settling with yourself that every man on earth who doesn't subscribe to your theory must perforce be " written down an ass."

We all ought to remember one most important thing about foxhunting: the easiest thing in the world is to spoil the sport. A man who *will* walk or, worse still, trot, his horse round a covert or through a ride, at inopportune moments, a woman who *will* give a little scream because a squirrel runs up a tree beside her, and Tommy, just home from school, who insists upon shouting to Billy, the other side of a copse, to inform him that " Pa said he musn't have the pony to-day, so he took it," are all distinct terrors to the Master and the rest of the field. Of course, we all know by heart the maxims taught us by our forbears as to never pressing hounds at a check, being careful never to head the fox, *cum multis aliis*, and to these, I think, we might usefully add one more—to keep quiet. Beckford tells the young sportsman *what* to holloa under given circumstances. With the big fields of modern days I would say, " Don't holloa at all ; " that is, of course, if you are not an experienced hand at the game. If you are, you don't want my advice or that of anyone else to guide you, but to a rider in his first season or so, I would say, " Keep your mouth rigidly closed and never seek to use your whip thong ; " in the same way that I should say to a man about to ride his first steeplechase—" Sit still," and consider it the most practical piece of admonition possible to give.

A thing which not only the young, but also the experienced amongst us, are painfully apt to forget, is never to lose sight of hounds from the moment they are thrown into covert. Neglect of this precaution often loses you so much start that you have to drive your horse to catch them, and so distress him that you cannot enjoy the spin when you *do* get up. If they go away very fast, the probability is that you don't catch them at all! This is an especially cheerful situation if you have travelled from town for the express purpose of hunting. When you do get well away with them, then try to "go into every field with the hounds," as the great Tom Smith recommended. That piece of advice calls to mind the story of the sporting old parson, who, encountering his Bishop at a ball, was by him taken to task for the "high crime and misdemeanour" of foxhunting.

"But," said the parson, "your Lordship, I see, goes to dances."

"Ah," replied the wily Bishop, "but I am never in the same room with the dancers."

"Well, my Lord," said the parson, with the suspicion of a twinkle in his eye, "my horse and I are both growing old, and we are never in the same field with the hounds!"

To my mind, a *really* good run is indeed a *rara avis*. It takes such an alarmingly large combination of circumstances to obtain—a good fox, a good country, a good scent; then that you shall be on a good horse and get a good start. Only one of these things may be lacking, and away goes all your enjoyment, but, granted all the requisites, bear in mind this axiom: having got well off in front, *keep there!* Foxhunting is essentially a sociable sport, and remembering this, we ought to pursue a give-and-take policy; not riding solely for ourselves, but having a due regard for others' comfort. There is no excuse for spoiling the sport, however much a man may talk about going out to please himself, &c. Such stuff savours not only of selfishness, but of "bounce" as well.

Of stone-wall countries I have a very slight experience, but have been told by those best qualified to judge, that they are not so formidable to ride over, as we, who know little about them, imagine. As a rule —almost an invariable one, I believe—there are no ditches on either side, and the great thing to be cautious of is that you do not land in a chalk-pit! Of course the best amongst stone-wall-country packs is that kept by the noble owner of Badminton, the Duke of Beaufort, to whom hunting men owe so much in a variety of ways. The Duke's great courtesy, and the goodness of heart he displays to his inferiors, are well known, and I, personally, have experienced such kindness and consideration at his hands as I shall not easily forget. The Heythrop, in some parts, have a good many walls to surmount. On the Gloucestershire side they get a good allowance of grass, and, in the other direction, much too large a supply of woodland.

The injuries caused to horses in failing to clear these obstacles, are usually of a severe nature, especially if they "knee" them at all. Some time since, hearing of a good horse who had struck a wall pretty hard in the Cheltenham country, I went down, and, finding the injury to the knee comparatively slight, bought him. His jumping powers at everything are undeniable, but he has never forgotten that it was a wall that " rose up and hit him," and nothing will induce him to leave less than a foot between himself and the top of any obstacle of the kind now, though it is nearly three years since his mishap.

The fashion of modern writing is to decry the horse, hound, and man of to-day, and always to elevate the celebrities of a bygone time at their expense. And this glorification of the past, is not confined to writing. Who is it that has not, at some time or other, been speaking of Cannon or Archer, and been immediately awed into silence with the mystic names of "Nat" and Jim Robinson? Who, again, has ever dared to mention the best cross-country riders of to-day, without having Osbaldeston and Sir Harry Goodricke fired off at him, by some pre-historic fossil, who goes on the principle that nothing is right except what took place in *his* day! Because horses don't run four-mile heats nowadays, it by no means follows that we have none at Newmarket that *could* accomplish those slightly dreary performances; and if the hounds of to-day don't, as a rule, make fifteen and twenty-mile points, there is a solid reason for it, quite apart from any question of decadence. The simple explanation is contained in the one word, *pace*. The horse that can gallop for a mile, at the speed required to win a Royal Hunt Cup, would make many of the old four-mile-heaters—could they be resuscitated—look extremely silly at the end of a race over the Newmarket Beacon Course, and the victor in the Liverpool Grand National, four and three-quarter miles, over about thirty big fences, and with some eleven or twelve stone on his back—a journey which is ordinarily accomplished under ten minutes—would have small difficulty in *losing* the old-fashioned, dock-tailed, half-bred, bestridden by our forefathers, in a run of any length, and over any country in the world! Horses are better *bred* than they used to be, they are faster, by far, than they were, and every child knows that the higher the pressure, the shorter time it can be kept up. Given a slightly decreased rate of speed, and our horses would be found not only as good, but better stayers, in my humble opinion, than any that have made themselves famous in a past age. The Frenchmen are pretty smart in securing our best staying blood, but they haven't got it *all* yet.

I think he would be a bold man who "stood" even the mighty Eclipse against Robert the Devil, over a two or three mile course, both coming to the post in their best form; and if Prince Charlie could have been matched over the Rowley Mile, with anything that ever saw the light before him, I, for one, should have been tempted to "have a dash," and a big one too, on the bonny chestnut son of Blair Athol!

Amongst the farmers over whose land hounds run, there is, in most countries, a very friendly feeling; and provided that riders know the difference between wheat and weeds, and use their heads in crossing the land, very little real harm is likely to result. We should never be guilty of little pieces of inconsiderate behaviour, such as passing through a gate and leaving it open behind us, when stock are in the field; knocking down sheep hurdles, or unnecessarily pulling fences about in order to get through, &c. Then, also, we must remember we hunt on sufferance, and that if a man objects to our riding over his land, he is quite within his strict rights, and we are bound to respect his prejudices. I recollect a pleasant little incident, in connection with this subject, in the Crawley and Horsham country. Our fox had gone straight across a big piece of wheat, whither the whole field followed him, and he was finally rolled over right on the owner's front lawn. In the midst of the "worry" the farmer came pounding along on his fat old horse, out of breath, and in a high state of excitement. The Master rode up to meet him, and said very courteously—

"I am very sorry, Mr. R—, I'm afraid we've cut your wheat about, very much."

"D—n the wheat, sir! Have you killed your fox?" was the panting and sportsmanlike reply.

CHAPTER III.

WITH STAGHOUNDS.

THE three principal packs of these hounds, the Queen's, Lord Rothschild's, and the Mid-Kent, are all within easy reach of the metropolis. The two former are pretty close to each other, on the Great Western and North - Western lines respectively. Some of the Queen's, and nearly all of Lord Rothschild's country, is excellent. These are both of them non-subscription packs. The Mid-Kent, when they get into the district round Sevenoaks, or near the kennels, in the immediate neighbourhood of Maidstone, enjoy some really fine spins, with plenty of grass and big fencing, but the country is not so good on the Farningham side. They meet at 12, and may be reached by either the South-Eastern, or London, Chatham, and Dover Railways. Essex is catered for by the Hon. H. Petre, and you have only to go either to Croydon or Redhill, if you are desirous of patronizing the Surrey. The Warnham are a little further afield, crossing the same country as the Crawley and Horsham Foxhounds. If, however, your soul soars above hunting the carted deer, you must repair to the West, and follow the Devon and Somerset over their wild and picturesque heather and moorland. It need hardly be remarked that this is *not* the pack for Londoners. It is rather the fashion to rave about the sport here, and, as every August comes round, the stereotyped rhodomontade is hurled at us, in the shape of an account of the opening day, probably penned in Fleet Street, by some enterprising youth, who, if he got on a horse one side, would be sure to fall off the other :—" Cloutsham "—" the old harbourer " — " warrantable deer " — " vast expanse of moorland "—" far-famed Dunkery Beacon "—" tufting "—" the wild Red Deer," &c., &c. All these are dragged out to do duty, year after year, and to people who have never seen the country, the prospect certainly seems entrancing. As to the beauty of the scenery, *that* is undeniable; but the newspaper paragraphist omits to mention, First: bogs, *ad libitum*. Secondly: scrambling over eternal boulders, and sliding down one hill, in order to clamber up another. Thirdly : no jumping ! All this is somewhat melancholy, and seriously detracts from the enjoyment of the fun. Still it is, without doubt, a soul-stirring thing to see hounds run here, and if, by carefully following *someone who knows*, you avoid getting bogged, miss breaking your neck over a boulder, and don't *always* find yourself at the bottom of one hill, when hounds have just reached the top of another, the very picturesqueness of the surroundings may make it well worth your while to pay this pack a visit. Native horses are the things to ride; most of them that have been bred on the moor are not to be *cajoled* into a bog. To a stranger going down into this country, no better advice could be given than that he should place himself in the hands of Mr. John White, of Taunton, who always has a large stud fit to go. I have never availed myself of his services in this country, but he has mounted me, right well, with the Blackmoor Vale, and I speak as I find.

As far as I have ever been able to see, a fresh deer has no particular choice as to whether he runs up wind or down; in fact, there is no calculating *how* they are going to run. It by no means follows that because they know the country, or because that country is an open Down, that they mean going; equally uncertain is it whether they will choose the hills, or the vales, and sometimes, in the stiffest-fenced countries, they will go as straight as a gun-barrel, for miles. These remarks apply as much to the wild, as to the carted deer. Even more than in foxhunting, therefore, should we stick tight to the hounds, if we wish to get to the end of a run at all; there is nothing upon which we may, with any safety, base our calculations in case of getting thrown out.

In the way of stratagem, a hunted deer, though giving pride of place to the "thief of the world," as friend Jorrocks calls him, is a very long way from a fool; as witness his prowess when he "runs to herd," *i.e.*, pushes up another deer and lies close himself, a plan that, of course, can only be pursued where the wild animal is hunted. A deer will often, also, manage to obliterate the scent by "taking soil," as getting to the water is called, though his principal object in doing this, is, undoubtedly, to refresh himself by his bath.

Nowhere can the hunting of the carted deer, in my humble opinion, be seen to such advantage as in the Vale of Aylesbury, following Lord Rothschild's pack, one of the very best extant. The thanks of all true sportsmen are due to the munificent master of Ascott for his unselfish conduct in maintaining this princely establishment in the style he does, and for affording so much enjoyment to the public, free of all cost to them. In Frederick Cox and Mark Howcott, the Hunt have two as able servants as it is possible to get, and in spite of the former's many and honourable scars, which have affected his seat on a horse, he still contrives to be with his hounds in their fastest spins. I believe Mark would ride at a furniture van, if necessity arose, and in that respect he reminds me strongly of George Loder, huntsman to the Crawley and Horsham, who created a profound impression upon me, on an occasion, some twelve years back, when at the finish of a hard run, he rammed the almost dead-beaten chestnut mare he was on, at about four feet six of stiff, new timber, and just won the deal!

I have already briefly alluded to the Vale of Aylesbury; it is one of the most essentially hunting and riding countries in the kingdom, and the fences are all that the heart of man could desire. Add to this, that it is, for the Londoner, extremely accessible by means of a goodly train service, and what more can we want?

The charge of "coming out to ride," in contradistinction to "coming out to hunt," is frequently levelled at followers of staghounds, and no doubt there is a good deal of truth in it; but those who indulge in unpleasant observations of this kind are usually men whose time is their own, and who can therefore afford a blank day, now and then, with foxhounds. But how about the busy man, snatching his day here and there, just as he gets the opportunity? A blank day comes very hard upon him, and this he obviates by going with staghounds. Besides this, the pursuit of the carted deer occasionally affords hounds an excellent chance of showing something more than galloping and staying power, and gives the huntsman as much real work to do as his brother of the vulpine chase. Of course, with fox-hunting enthusiasts, such as Mr. Jorrocks, we can expect no quarter in discussing what that distinguished sportsman likened to "turning out a hass, and 'unting 'im," but then we are not all as intolerant as the worthy grocer. I have just been talking to-day to a good sportsman of the olden type, a friend of the ever-to-be-lamented Rev. "Jack" Russell. He was in the habit of staying with the celebrated Parson, for the stag-hunting, and, joined by Mr. Granville Somerset, no less famed for his prowess across country, than for his powers at the Parliamentary Bar, the trio must have formed a right merry party at dinner, after their healthful day upon the purple heather. My friend has hunted with most packs, both of fox and staghounds, and nothing, in his opinion, comes up to the chase of the red deer, whether on the Quantocks or across Exmoor.

One of the funniest things I ever remember in connection with the sport, happened some years ago, whilst going in a run with the Old Surrey Foxhounds. We had been running somewhere about twenty minutes, when, in getting through some woodland, about half-a-dozen of us went down a ride, and soon after emerging therefrom I came in view of the hounds running hard. Pushing my horse a bit, I got up to the front rank, and immediately after we came to the top of a hill. Judge of my intense astonishment when I saw, away to the left, a *deer*, with the pack in hot pursuit! We had actually changed packs in the woodland, and I had unwittingly followed the staghounds, and let my own pack go!

I never had the opportunity of seeing

Lord Wolverton's bloodhounds, but have learnt from those who have, what a rare treat it was to watch them at work. The head of the Glyns has sold them now, and started a pack of harriers in their place. Speaking of the Glyn family, one cannot help remembering how well Sir Richard of that ilk has deserved of Somerset and Dorset men for the able way in which, for seventeen years, he discharged the duties of Master to the Blackmoor Vale, spending enormous sums on the pack out of his own pocket, and less than two years since I had the pleasure of seeing him going, as well as ever, with these hounds. He could not have resigned them into better hands than those of Mr. Merthyr Guest, the present Master, whose ability is no less remarkable than the never-failing courtesy he extends to "all sorts and conditions of men" who hunt with him.

The paddock-fed deer seldom exhibits much fear when uncarted before hounds. Plenty of them, in fact, have to be fairly driven away from the field they are turned out in, and even then, go away at a leisurely trot. Properly trained, by being hustled round the paddock regularly every day, the lady gives as good runs as her lord, who would often be a nasty customer for the huntsman and whips to tackle, if not bereft of his antlers. Even as it is, they can often make a very spirited resistance to the "take," and the inexperienced had better be chary of offering assistance in the process, to the hunt servants. Such, at all events, is the advice feelingly given by a gentleman whose zeal exceeded his discretion, a little time ago, and who was vigorously forwarded into a cucumber frame, by way of reminder, for his pains!

Some runs of staghounds of late years

have been a trifle astonishing for their duration, and how horses and hounds can keep going for four hours or more, at a stretch, is mystifying. The deer Moonlight, a celebrated customer pertaining to the Mid-Kent pack, was uncarted about 12 one day, two or three seasons ago, and was not taken till eight o'clock at night! One horse, I believe, comprised the "field" at the finish, and how *he* got there is a puzzle! It is no unusual thing for a run of twenty to thirty miles to be chronicled, and with Captain Kerr's pack, in the County Down, there are one or two even longer than that, on record. The old Norfolk staghounds used to get some lengthy gallops over a capital country. The 19th Hussars, fresh from their Egyptian glories, have now taken them over, and may good luck attend the conjunction of capital sportsmen and a right good pack.

In concluding this chapter, let me pay a slight tribute of respect to poor Dawkins, who had, only shortly before, come to hunt the Surrey staghounds, when he met with his death by his horse coming back on him. An abler, more civil and well-conducted hunt servant did not exist, and both in the field and in his private life he left a character and example that were, as he, poor fellow, was, across a country, "hard to beat."

CHAPTER IV.

WITH DRAGHOUNDS.

"PEOPLE who ride with the Drag amply prove their title to trespass on the hospitality of the local Lunatic Asylum," said a first-rate cross-country rider, sententiously, one day when the subject was being hotly debated, and the observation sank all the deeper into my mind from the fact that, for years, I have been an ardent follower in "the pursuit of the red herring" myself. Dearly as I have got to love this afternoon scurry, much as one enjoys the fun of racing over the grass, and charging the somewhat formidable fences that are invariably crossed by the human runner, I must confess to thinking that after a man has passed the "forties," he would do well to take to some rather less exciting pastime. It is the best game in life for bachelors to play at, but if a man has a family depending on his exertions, it might be better that he should give up anything so likely to necessitate a coroner's inquest.

"It's steeplechasing," says one, contemptuously. So it is, practically, my friend, and steeplechasing, let me say, is about as pretty a sport as a young man need wish for. Drag-hunting has one advantage over steeplechasing, too, by no means to be lost sight of; there is no money depending on your horse, and, therefore, you can just pull him up whenever he gets beaten, without the consequence of having mud (both literal and metaphorical) thrown at you, as you ride back into the paddock !

I believe the proportion of falls got, out with Draghounds, is something like twenty, to the one, incurred with other packs. This, of course, arises chiefly from the pace; there is no time, generally speaking, to pull your horse back and let him take his own time at the fences. You must send him along from end to end, and unless he either flies everything, or has got the pace of a Derby winner to make up lost time on the flat, you very soon find yourself " out of it."

There are a few packs of these hounds within easy reach of London, but, as far as I know, they are all in private hands. I suppose the best known are those belonging to the Household Brigade, near Windsor, and the smart little pack owned by the Royal Artillerymen at Woolwich. Chiefly with a view to the farmers' interests, their meets are kept strictly private, and, as a rule, a very select field is the result. Thank goodness for it, say I! If we had a hundred horsemen charging the first fence together, jealous as girls, and each trying to get a good start, it would really come cheaper in the end to have an undertaker attached to the Hunt, at an inclusive salary!

Many of the advantages offered by stag-hunting, are also obtainable here, such, for instance, as being sure of your gallop, no waiting about covert, &c., and the late hour of starting — frequently not till three o'clock—is, of course, unique. A mistake is often made, I think, in choosing a "rasper" for the first obstacle. Were it done with the object of shaking off a crowd, sifting the chaff from the wheat, it would be understandable, but with the very small number who usually assemble for the gallop, this cannot be—yet it is almost invariably done. A horse can't be expected to jump at the first go off, as he will do later on; he has not warmed to the work, or perhaps he is of an excitable temperament, and the sight of the refusing, rearing, and kicking crowd of his fellows—there is generally this little performance going on at the first fence—upsets his nerves, and then what happens?—there is more scrimmaging, and we see, oh frequent occurrence! that Mr. Eager, whose horse refused the first time, turns him short round at it again, without letting Captain Shortemper have *his* chance first. The consequence is that amidst the din of tongues, amidst the whipping and spurring, an ominous "thud" announces a collision.

"D—n it, sir! where the devil are you going!" shout both the excited sportsmen, simultaneously, at each other. A third then gallops up and gets over; then another comes at it, a bit too fast, his horse slips on taking off, and "an imperial crowner" into the next field is the result. The huntsman, whip, and half a dozen more of us have already got nearly down to the next obstacle, a flight of post and rails. One after the other we all manage to negotiate them, our leader landing on knees and nose; but scrambling up again, without a scratch, he keeps his place at the head of affairs, and, sailing gaily away again, sends his horse at, and surmounts, a quickset and ditch on the far side. The said ditch claims its victim in the shape of the fourth man essaying it. The last we see of the mishap, after discovering that he is not hurt, is his horse's four legs waving aimlessly about in the air. Hounds are still racing away in front, and putting a longer distance than ever between themselves and the nearest of the horsemen. There is no baffling of scent to contend with here, and nothing that need hold their noses down for a second; all they have to do is to *gallop!* Now we begin to rise a slight hill, which rapidly brings our leader's flashy, non-staying weed, back to us, and a stiff-built, powerful little chestnut, who has been plodding doggedly along in the rear of the first flight, immediately goes to the head of affairs. On the summit of the incline we are confronted by a forbidding looking, stubbly hedge, which the gallant chestnut at once proceeds to tackle. Judiciously taking a slight pull at him, his rider catches him hard by the head and sends him at the weakest place. Well, there isn't *much* to spare, but he gets to the other side " all standing!" Three others get over in safety, but the severity of the pace has been too much for the rest, most of whom either fall or decline the business altogether.

At a reduced pace, we go on over the next field, and then, turning right-handed, descend a long piece of stubble, jump a low rail, and heave in sight of the one obstacle that now divides us from the ever-welcome "check." This said obstacle is a formidable-looking brook, about sixteen feet of open water. We are going to it downhill, so are not afraid to push our somewhat blown horses to an increased pace as we approach it. The first man gets over, the second comes clean in, the third succeeds, with a flourish and one hind leg dropped in, and the next two refuse point blank. Hounds have already stopped where the drag has been lifted, and, puffing and panting, we slip off our horses, who, with heads down, flanks heaving, and tails distended, are only too thankful for the breather. Some minutes elapse before the first of the stragglers appears over the brow of the hill; the hoof-marks on the wet ground, and—shall we confess it?—the ominous gaps, here and there, in the fences, have effectually marked our track, and shown him the way we came. Seeing hounds at a standstill, he, like a wise man, declines the brook, and crosses by the little low bridge, higher up the stream. Some half-dozen more eventually arrive; the rest have either given it up, or the line has proved a "stopper" for them.

Refreshed by the halt, hounds are slowly moved off again. We jog along half a mile of road, and then, turning in at a gate, start across a big bit of pasture, rather holding, but splendid going for all that. We are bearing away to the left now, and the first thing that bars our progress is a real stiff quickset, something that you instinctively rise in your stirrups to have a look over, directly you come within range. "Nothing the other side," we murmur to ourselves, thankfully, and then Number One crams his hat down on his head and charges it. Number One may have meant to get over it, but Number One's horse distinctly *didn't!* His refusal causes the next man's animal to whip round, too, and then one old hunter, fired all round, and who couldn't trot on the hard road to save his life, cocks his ears forward and gallops right between the refusers, topping the hedge in splendid style; with his lead, two more get over, and are soon joined on the far side by most of the others, who have galloped up the hedgerow to an open gate. Surmounting an easy flight of hurdles, we find ourselves in a field which gives us the choice, by way of egress, of a high hog-backed stile, a five-barred gate, and a rasping blackthorn hedge. One man goes for the gate, but, unfortunately, the gate retaliates and "goes for" him, turning him over in real business-like fashion. Nobody seems to fancy the stile, but one adventurous sportsman comes at the blackthorn at about forty miles an hour; neither he nor his horse see a stiff rail that is run through it, and which catches the latter's near hind leg, with the effect of hanging them up, struggling head downwards, for several seconds, until the timber snaps across and lets them into the next field "knees and nose." However, it has tunnelled a way through for the rest, who follow without a moment's delay.

Then come three or four enjoyable, *breakable* fences; the grass here is all sound going, and the pace a racing one. An open ditch looms in sight; down we go at it! It *is* a big one! Two men are racing for the honour of being first at it, and charge it almost abreast; result, one in, the other over. Following them much too closely, the next—a youth who labours under the delusion that he can ride—unable to pull up, literally jumps ditch, horse and man together, and after landing safely, promptly falls over his horse's head, and takes up a position on his back, admirably adapted to the study of astronomy. "Thank goodness *he's* down," murmurs an old hand, as he lets in the Latchfords and clears the obstacle in safety. "I never feel my neck's safe with that young ass careering all over the place!" Three others get over, and then we sit down in our saddles to make the best of our way to where the pack have already finished the spin. A flight of hurdles and an unsubstantial rail, which is chested and smashed by the foremost horse, brings us to our journey's end.

The huntsman, leaving his smoking steed to take care of himself—he won't stray very far after this, depend on it!—fetches the paunch from the runner's cart, and, after a blast or two on the horn, distributes the spoil. Whilst the hounds devour it, we light our cigars and look out for the stragglers. We, who happen to have had the best of the luck to-day, are, of course, feeling an inward superiority to the rest of mankind, that we wouldn't part with for a five-pound note! Here comes one man with a dirty coat, talking to another who has broken a stirrup leather. Why, it's our friend Shortemper, chatting in most amicable fashion with Mr. Eager! They are fastest of friends again, and now the latter takes one of the gallant captain's proffered Cabanas. They are overtaken by a riderless horse, whose bridle has broken and come off. His groom, who has just appeared on the scene, will have an exciting, if laborious, half-hour's work before catching him. Three more closely follow, each explaining that had he been on some-*thing* else he would have finished some*where* else. Then, in the far distance, appears a man leading his horse, which has broken down in front. We don't wait any longer, but with a cheery " Good-night!" jog quietly off, on our respective homeward journeys, each hugging himself with the idea that he, individually, has had a bit the best of it, and mentally resolving that *his* particular horse is "worth his weight in gold." Next time we go out we shall probably get " pounded " at something or other, and then say that we would "sell him for a tenner!" Such is life, and such are the ways of hunting men!

The rustics, who congregate round the jumps, are a terrible nuisance sometimes, with their shouting and yelling, enough to make any young or nervous horse "turn it up" at once. Then, when he has satisfactorily brought about the refusal, Chawbacon is thoroughly delighted, and indulges in unlimited derision. I remember a scene of the kind at a big brook once. "You'll fall in, gov'ner," shrieked the yokel, grinning all round the back of his head at his own witticism. "Yes, I should if it was anything like as big as your mouth is," was the prompt reply, and thereupon did the said yokel "curl up" and retire, amidst the merciless laughter of the crowd. They are ever too ready, also, to block up every practicable place in a fence with their unwelcome presence, and to increase the size of a jump whenever it lies in their power so to do.

Draghunting, at its worst, is a very pleasant substitute for the real thing, and in case no pack of regular hounds is within reach, or where the country is a bad one, it is especially acceptable. In a country that is bad for natural hounds, you may often get a small Leicestershire, by means of the human runner, who, of course, eschews the plough, and takes every bit of grass land possible. He also has the option of the fences, and can choose those only with a fair take off and no traps. Then, again, in a "wired" district, the track being known beforehand, the little white flags give you friendly warning of where you may dispense with the "nippers," and jump with comparative safety. The worst part of the whole business seems to me to lie in the harm it undoubtedly does the horses, on account of the butchering way they have to be ridden. Big fence after big fence has to be faced, at a pace more like racing than hunting, and I have seen countless good horses turn cowards after a season of this work. Indeed, I cannot call to mind a single animal that was ever any use for the game after his third season at it. To those who argue that it is no worse than steeplechasing for them, I would say that the steeplechase horse rarely has to gallop more than three miles over fences, and also that he is not called upon, as a rule, to do this, anything like twice a week throughout the season. To my mind, the best of all mounts, for this sport, is a steeplechaser who has got a bit too slow to win races, but has, with that very slowness, become pleasant and temperate at his fences; he has the pace to keep in front without distressing himself, and can cover plenty of ground at his leaps. If, however, you *must* choose between a slow horse that is a certainty at his fences, or one with any amount of speed, but an unreliable jumper, don't hesitate a moment, but take the former by all manner of means. As a general rule, there is so much jumping to be done, in this style of riding to hounds, that refusals are too serious to be compensated for by mere speed on the flat. There is no better school for getting a steeplechaser fit to run, and giving him some jumping practice at the same time. Talking of that subject reminds me of a spin I once rode in with Draghounds, when we had some " top-sawyers," in the steeplechasing way, forming the major part of the starters, and for " quality " in the riding line, I have only to mention that, included in the twelve or fifteen who composed the field, were Mr. W. H. Moore, Mr. Harry Beasley, and another less known but quite as able a gentleman rider ; John Jones and Arthur Hall, the Epsom steeplechase professionals, I think C. Lawrence, one of the ablest of cross-country jockeys, and two or three more of the same type, whose names have escaped my memory. I don't think there was one there who had not ridden in silk! *That* field was a comparatively safe one to ride in. No fear of Inexperience jumping on top of you there! I *have* seen a man, off his horse on the top of a bank, the animal being fairly bogged in the adjoining open ditch, have his velvet cap (he was hunting the hounds) taken off by the next man, who almost jumped over him! That sort of thing is just a little too exciting for peaceful enjoyment! I myself have been knocked almost out of the saddle by an impetuous youth, who just missed jumping on top of me, by a miracle. It afforded me, I am bound to confess, a calm and tranquil satisfaction to see that the result was an "imperial crowner" for the aggressor, who so humbly apologized, however, that I relented and caught his horse for him! It really was too close a thing to be pleasant. I lost one stirrup iron, and was shunted so far out of the saddle that I had to hang on, like a fly to a ceiling, half over the next field.

Very few of the fair sex, as may be imagined, come out with draghounds, and I think they are wise. Still, the few I have seen go with them at all, have gone right gallantly. One in especial, whom I had the honour of piloting throughout one season, I once saw jump an obstacle of mixed timber and "quick," over five feet in height, with a drop on the other side, on a cob that could walk under the standard at 14.3.

Nothing puts a man out of conceit with himself so much as going with these hounds. The best of jumpers will occasionally refuse, or fall, going the pace they do over what is, practically, an unprepared steeplechase course. Then it is that the men who secretly hug themselves with the idea that they "can get to hounds on anything"—and their name is legion—find themselves so grievously humiliated. A refusal, unless you can get your horse round and over at the next attempt, is almost as fatal to your chance here as it would be in a steeplechase, and therefore it continually happens that many of the crack men out, find themselves lobbing in at the finish, with the ruck. This, repeated two or three times, will convince a man that, ride he "never so wisely," he is but mortal after all!

CHAPTER V.

WITH HARRIERS.

No better example of *how* harriers should be handled could be found than in Mr. Fellowes's celebrated pack, the Shotesham, near Norwich. A good banking country, plenty of hares, friendly landowners, an unusually smart lot of hounds, and, above all, Mr. Fellowes himself, constitute an amalgam of attraction for the hound-lover, not often to be met with. Some of the hares here, run like foxes, and give just as good sport. An ideal huntsman, the Master still slips over a country in wonderful fashion, not, truly, as of yore, when he was wont to make the hardest of them cry "enough" in the grass countries, but riding slowly at everything, never hurrying, but always being *there!*

Well do I mind me of my first introduction to this pack. I was young, on a strange horse—such a beast!—and had never ridden in a banking country before. Consequently, when my mount persistently declined to fly the obstacles, my supreme ignorance prompted me—never dreaming that banking should be done *slowly!*—to ram him at everything at forty-miles-an-hour pace. The result was, of course, inevitable! Over we all came in the most approved fashion—unluckily for me, horse being on top!—and by the time I recovered enough of my senses to know one end of the animal from the other, the hounds must have been about a mile this side of the North Pole!

In spite of Mr. Jorrocks's severe remark that "I never sees a man a-trudgin' along a turnpike with a thick stick in 'is 'and and a pipe in 'is mouth, but I says to myself, 'There goes a man well mounted for 'arriers'"—there is no better school, from a really hunting point of view, for youngsters than this. Here they can pick up the method of hunting, the canons of that great mystery, scent, and such invaluable things as not pressing hounds, and being patient under all circumstances, far better than they could acquire them with more rapidly working packs, because time is given them to see, and work things out for themselves. Again, after a man passes that time of life when other hounds go a bit too fast for him, I venture to say that no pleasure in this way is greater than watching harriers at their work. Do not let it be supposed, for a moment, that I would relegate harriers to those, in either their first, or second childhood. Such a thought is far from my mind; still I presume there are few men the sunny side of fifty, who would prefer a day with them, to a spin with foxhounds. Hares *will* run rings for the most part, though here and there you do get a straight-necked one—still, it must be confessed, these latter are rather the exception than the rule. The present huntsman of Mr. Lubbock's harriers, the redoubtable " Jack," will tell you that a Kentish hare, capable of standing fifty minutes or an hour, before hounds, is no uncommon thing, and the pack has for many years shown excellent sport in a rather bad country, both in its present ownership and when kept by that sterling sportsman, Mr. George Russell, of Plumstead, to whom, with his equally well-known brothers, hunting men in West Kent owe so much.

There is one thing we are all rather apt to overlook, and that is, that farmers are much more sorely tried by harriers, than by any other hounds. In the nature of things, the former will often cross and recross a field, perhaps of seeds, roots, or wheat, a dozen times, where the latter traverse it but once. For this reason we ought to be doubly careful of the way we ride, so as to do as little damage as possible. For the enthusiastic schoolboy, magnificent opportunities are lavishly given for jumping unnecessary fences, a performance that he can execute with the consoling reflection, that, after he has consistently fallen off at each, there will be plenty of time for him to resume the perpendicular before hounds have got very far away.

In drawing for a hare, not only do the hounds scatter widely, but the field is also supposed to transform itself into an auxiliary pack and assist. In spite of all endeavours to "rouse him," however, I am quite confident that many a hare has been literally walked over, and never put up, so closely do they lie. Generally speaking, these hounds do not hunt a hedgerow as thoroughly as they should; if they do, they usually put in a little rabbiting on their own account, which is distinctly not in the programme. I have seen it suggested, somewhere, that terriers might be used for this purpose, but while agreeing that they would do the work better, I fear that trouble would arise from the quarrelsome nature of harriers, and there would also be some difficulty in getting terriers to keep up with them when they run. The experiment of hunting hare with foxhounds is a failure; they have too much dash and are too impetuous for the work. A harrier's greatest virtue is patience, and an ability to hunt without human assistance. It must have struck many how strangely alike a hare and a bagged fox will run, the latter not knowing the country, and perhaps his having been some time in captivity accounts for this, and for choice, a pack of harriers would give much better sport with such a quarry than a pack of foxhounds. Not that I would venture to insinuate that my readers are likely to indulge in such a mongrel entertainment as hunting a bagman. A tom-cat would generally give about as much sport!

I do not think I have ever been out with half a dozen different packs of harriers in my life, although I have acted as whip to two, and I frankly confess that I should take them only when other hounds are not within reach. To me, the most interesting incident which ever occurred, in connection with harriers, was when a great friend of mind put his horse at a fence, fell clean over it, and came down on his nose. Upon rising to his feet and rubbing the offended organ with rueful countenance, he was greeted with this consoling remark from the irate owner of the field into which he had so unfortunately landed, "Get out o' this, will 'ee? Ware wheat then!" "And considering," said the unhappy victim to me, afterwards, "that all I'd done to his beastly wheat was to plough it up with my nose, I think it *was* rather rough upon me!"

CHAPTER VI.

STEEPLECHASING AND HURDLE-RACING.

FOR "pretty" sport, one might go a long way before being able to beat the sight of half a dozen crack steeplechase horses sweeping down, almost abreast, at one of their jumps. To hear the quick thunder of the hoofs, the hard breathing of the horses, mingled with the hard swear—I mean, speaking—of the riders, is enough to make the blood stir and tingle in any human being, except, perhaps, the "professional beauty," who I once saw, at Goodwood, deliberately put up her sunshade and turn her back on the finish of a race! Most decent riders to hounds entertain the curious idea that they are well fitted to ride in steeplechases. As far as the fencing is concerned, they are doubtless not far wrong, but a good deal more than that is wanted in order to become a successful pilot "between the flags." Judgment of pace, and that indescribable something known as "hands," which I always think means a sort of intuitive perception of what your horse is doing, and what nature of assistance, if any, he stands in need of from his rider, a feeling which is, or ought to be, instinct in the fingers. True that the hunting man *should* know these things, but the jockey *must*. Then again the tricks —I use the word in its best sense—of race-riding, the use of the whip with either hand, and above all the iron nerve and cool calculating head, are not given to many a man who can, and does, go right well at the tail of a pack of hounds. In hurdle-racing I think there is even more in jockeyship, and the clever way in which men like Mr. E. P. Wilson will half jump, half rush a horse over the obstacles, must have been noticed by all observant race-goers. A steeplechase rider should always be a strong man on a horse, and this by no means depends on whether he is a powerfully-built man, in reality. Plenty of men of wretched physique, light and weedy in appearance, would not be in the least distressed, and would be well able to hold a big, awkward horse together, at the finish of a three or four mile steeplechase, where the more stoutly made one would be rolling about helplessly in his saddle, unable to get an ounce out of his mount. Being powerful on a horse seems to be a happy combination of hands, good condition, courage, and general "knack."

Never shall I forget the finish of a two and a half mile steeplechase in which I was riding, and where the race was fairly thrown away by the inexperienced jockey of the second. He was helplessly endeavouring to use his whip, letting his horse at the same time, sprawl all over the course, and with his mount going twice as fast as the winner, he was beaten a short head! Had he taken example by his conqueror's demeanour—an experienced jockey, who sat as still as a mouse, merely riding his horse with his hands—he must have won by many a length! The best thing for the amateur to do is to train *himself*. He requires it, just as much as the animal he is going to ride. This was the plan adopted by Lord Manners in 1882 when he won the Grand National at Liverpool, on Seaman, by a head, after a desperate finish with Mr. Tom Beasley on Cyrus. Where would he have been had be not been as *fit* as he was? The verdict *must* have been reversed, and victory would have rested with his more practised opponent, over such a long, trying course. This win, by the way, must have been very galling to the owners of the second, considering that they had sold the winner, not long previously, out of their own stable.

The "gentlemen" have more than held their own against the professionals, in this greatest of cross-country contests, during the past few years. Mr. "Thomas," with Anatis, The Lamb, and Pathfinder; Mr. T. Beasley, with Empress and Woodbrook, a reputed roarer; Lord Manners on Seaman; Mr. J. M. Richardson, with a brace in consecutive years, Disturbance—Commotion's best son—and Reugny; Mr. E. P. Wilson, with Voluptuary and the ill-tempered Roquefort; Mr. F. G. Hobson, with one of the best horses that ever won, Austerlitz ; and Count Kinsky on Zoedone, all occur to the mind.

The innovation of the open ditch has not found favour on the part of owners and riders, and either with or without the guard rail, I cannot regard it as being anything like what its advocates claim for it : a fair hunting jump. Going at it at the pace they do, steeplechase horses are very liable to gallop almost into it before they see it at all, and I remember some time back at Sandown Park standing beside an open ditch without a rail, and seeing a horse literally gallop into it, and disappear from view ! Things are better now, it is true, in that the ditches are made shallow, instead of deep, but anyhow, to take these jumps at racing pace is a proceeding fraught with danger, and it is difficult to see what useful purpose can be served by retaining them. Most men found quite sufficient excitement in steeplechase riding without these "open graves," and I, for one, should be glad to see them abolished, and a "double" substituted. Should these lines catch the eye of any of the merry little party who went down to Esher, to ride at the first steeplechase meeting there, I wonder if he will remember the cheerful observation of one of the officials, who informed us, with great gusto, that "a surgeon was in readiness at the stand, and an ambulance waggon would be in attendance, in case ——" It was well meant, no doubt; still it takes a somewhat keen sense of humour on the part of jockeys about to ride to appreciate the unconsciously grim joke of the thing, at the time.

Mention of this excellently conducted meeting reminds one of the sad death of poor Mr. Greville Nugent ("Mr. St. James"), one of the pluckiest and best of cross-country riders. Many of us remember how, on one occasion, in riding Melita, he broke his leg against a post, but persevered to the end of the race, in the gamest fashion, and was only just beaten into second place at the finish. If there be any such thing, in reality, as luck, poor Greville Nugent had the cruellest, in his last fall. Riding in a Selling steeplechase, he came down, quite clear of his horse, Longford, and was rising unhurt from the ground, when a horse struck him with his forefoot, right on the base of the skull, and killed him. He was "all heart and no peel" with a vengeance! I believe he never turned the scale at eight stone in his life.

Provided that a man does not fall on his head, there does not seem much fear of serious injury in this sport, except from the horse. Very few men get hurt if they can keep clear of their own and other people's horses; in not being able to do so, undoubtedly, lies the danger. To find one's-self down, with an animal on top of one, is an extremely trying situation! Some years ago a steeplechase horse fell and then rolled completely over me, without breaking a bone. "Not a bad get off," thought I to myself afterwards, and with the exception of being severely cut about the head and one leg, and having a general vague idea that someone had been amusing himself by passing the garden roller over my much flattened carcase, I sustained no hurt at all. A capital plan it is—when practicable—to immediately cover your head and face with your arms, so as to escape injury, as far as may be, there.

There would be fewer bad falls if men, when they find their horses hopelessly beaten, would have the moral courage to pull them up, and not persevere. I know that the jeers of even the ignorant jackasses who hardly know a horse from a cow, and certainly have no clear perception of whether an animal is "done" or not, are not pleasant to bear, but surely it is preferable to thus run the gauntlet, than to cruelly press your horse and endanger your own neck? Young Goodwin probably lost his life through driving a blown horse at a fence, instead of ceasing to persevere, able and steady horseman as he was. Poor fellow! he lay for eleven or twelve days in the Grand Stand at Sandown, without moving a muscle, before he died. One cannot help admiration for his pluck, but *cui bono?* Of course, it is different to hunting; other people's money and other people's interests are concerned, and all must have weight with the rider. Now, in hunting, when a horse is beaten, it is sheer brutality to butcher him along after his sobbing sides have plainly told you the tale of his distress; nothing is involved except his rider's pleasure, and if the rider can get "pleasure" out of his good horse's sufferings, I do not think the community would be the losers if he *did* break his neck!

About as unpleasant a ride as a man can have, fell to my lot some time since, and thinking of it always brings a laugh up again, though I somehow failed to appreciate the joke at the time. It was in a Maiden steeplechase, and the day was more than diabolical. Snow was falling slightly, half the course was frozen and the other half "slush"; still, by laying straw, &c., on the landing side of the jumps, racing was considered practicable —by the stewards, who didn't have to ride. Shivering down to the post in thin silk jackets, with numb, blue fingers and—by way of pleasing contrast—red noses, we waited about for the starter, who had apparently been mislaid. By the time this important functionary turned up (wiping his mouth with the back of his hand, and smelling suspiciously of cloves!) horses' coats were all sticking up the wrong way, and I am afraid the riders' tempers were all "sticking up the wrong way," too! However, at last we did get off, and down to the first fence, where every horse in the field refused. I was lucky enough to get mine over first, and went on with a long lead. Jumping the fence on the far side, my hair fairly stood on end to see that *a plough* had been left, with grossest carelessness, so close that we landed within a yard of it! I managed to keep my mount in front till over the final obstacle, and from that point to the finish I had, perhaps, as hard work—physically, I mean

—as it would be possible to compress into the time. My horse was one of the slow, staying sort, but game as a pebble; the finish was up a stiff hill, and the only man I had to beat almost lying on me. I dared not use my whip, and all I could do was to sit down and drive him home to the best of my ability. By the time I got there (just a short head in front) I was not inclined to complain of the cold; rather was I requiring to be pegged up on a clothes line, and hung out to dry!

It is only since commencing this chapter that poor Fred Archer's brief span of life has come to a tragic close. He was a wonderful example of a weakly man on foot, but perhaps the most powerful jockey ever seen on a horse, not even excepting Custance, a really splendid cross-country rider, by the way. In connection with Archer, I remember well that Derby day in 1877, when the horses galloped past me, as I stood at the Paddock gate. The race was over, and I called to the great jockey to know who had won. White as death, he pointed to himself, indicating, as he swept past, that he was too breathless to speak. Directly he pulled his horse up (Silvio), he turned and, addressing me, said, " I've won." I asked " How far ? " and he replied " A head or a neck, I think," and then rode back to scale. It was his first Blue Riband win, and gained, most fittingly, in the colours of the man who had made his fortunes, more than anyone else, Lord Falmouth. A tragic and curious circumstance in connection with this incident is, that, of the friend I was with that day, Archer, and myself, all three comparatively young men, the premier jockey and my unfortunate friend have since died, both by their own hands, and both by bullet wounds.

Asking my reader's pardon for this somewhat gloomy digression, I turn to the subject of education. Don't shudder; I do not intend by that expression to mean the discussion of School Board statistics; I refer to the kind of education that converted Emblem, Lord Coventry's famous mare, from a bad refuser, into a winner of the Liverpool. I do not think a more striking instance of the efficacy of this education can be found, than in calling to mind the very recent case of Voluptuary. Mr. E. P. Wilson bought this horse, at a sale of "rubbish" by Lord Rosebery, for the sum of £150. The sale was effected during the second October meeting at Newmarket, and the following March, starting at a very remunerative price, the son of Cremorne negotiated the big course without putting a foot wrong, and won easily, Mr Wilson himself being in the saddle. "Quick horse and clever teacher," in this case ; and I do not think there are many instances on record to beat it. Mr. Garrett Moore, I remember, effected a marvellous improvement, some years since, with the savage Furley. Furley, a nice-looking colt by Honiton, I saw win the big steeplechase at Croydon, when he was five years old, Mr. J. M. Richardson up. At that time the horse jumped freely and well, but soon after he turned a perfect " pig," and would not look at his fences. A little later, he passed into the hands of the redoubtable " Garry," and, somehow or another, he effected quite a reformation with him ; he came out afterwards, and won several steeplechases, amongst them the big race at Croydon again, this time ridden by his trainer. He had not to do much on this occasion, it is true, beyond standing up, but that was more than seven out of his eight or nine opponents could manage, in consequence of the awful condition of the course.

Two very unpromising things to make first-class steeplechasers, judging by their initiatory performances, were the famous sisters, Emblem and Emblematic, both subsequently Grand National winners. One, I forget which, declined to jump even a little ditch, and always walked into it, only to be driven out again by a man with a whip! To put it mildly, this was not a cheerful beginning, yet we see what judicious education made of them. Congress, who was afterwards one of the finest jumpers ever seen on a race course, had to be pulled over his fences by men with cart ropes; and it was not until poor Sam Daniels' life had been lost in schooling Thunder, that the big chestnut would jump hurdles properly, though he afterwards took to it kindly enough.

Thoroughbred ones learn quickest, *pace* that great authority Whyte-Melville, who rather inclined to the opinion that they are more troublesome to teach than the cocktails. The circus ring-masters think otherwise, however, and for what are known as trick horses they almost invariably go to the racing stables. A few years back I was strolling through Sanger's stables at Norwich, when the ever popular and famous show was visiting the Cathedral town, and came across an old race-course friend, the costly Somerset. I am afraid to trust my memory to the extent of saying how many thousands his owner was supposed to be out of pocket over him altogether, but it was something very large, and he passed into Mr. Sanger's possession for twenty-six guineas! The poor old chap was looking fat and well, though naturally *minus* the bright, lustrous bloom I remember on him that Derby day when, with Custance up, he ran very fast, but had had enough of it a long way from home.

Most of our best horses on the flat are gifted with good looks. Here and there one finds the exception that proves the rule, but casting a hurried glance back over the " giants " of recent years, we find that such as Prince Charlie—fastest of " milers " —Cremorne, Doncaster, Marie Stuart, Isonomy, Petronel, Wheel of Fortune, Springfield, Peter, Bend Or, Robert the Devil, Melton, Ormonde, and The Bard were, or are, all handsome horses. Gladiateur was certainly an exception to the rule, and a good story is told of a friend of Mr. Tom Jennings's, in connection with the Derby-winner's appearance. Meeting the celebrated trainer one morning, the friend, whom we will call A., said —

" Well, Tom, have you got any ' rips '

you want to get rid of, at about £20, that'll do to run in harness?"

"Yes, I have," said Jennings; "come along in."

Having adjourned to the stables, they entered a loose-box, and the trainer told a boy to strip the horse standing in it.

"Oh, here, you know," said A., in tones of deep disgust, "you're not going to ask me £20 for that three-cornered-looking brute? What's his name, boy?"

"Gladiateur, sir!" replied the astonished youth.

However, although most good ones on the flat are good-looking, the rule by no means seems to apply to cross-country performers; and some of the best have been "mean-looking little beggars," as a famous jockey once described them. Casse-Tête, who won the Grand National of 1872, was an under-sized, weak-looking little chestnut mare, but her stamina was undeniable. Page, her jockey, however, had to use his whip heavily to keep her on her legs, coming over the last hurdles. Lord Coventry's celebrated brace of winners, Emblem and Emblematic, were very mean-looking. Shifnal and Pathfinder were a long way from handsome, and The Lamb—grandest and gamest of steeplechasers—was little more than a pony.

Two of the most unlikely horses to win steeplechases that I have ever had to do with were The Crow, by Flying Dutchman, and Lord Waldegrave, by Orlando, from Marionette, by Stockwell. The former carried me to hounds for a season, and a better—provided one could hold him—no man need wish for. Never did he turn his head from anything if you would let him have it at his own pace—about that of an express train!—yet the horse could never carry ten stone with comfort in his life! He would fairly bend under eleven, and yet he won several steeplechases with upwards of twelve stone on his back; *how*, I never could understand. Lord Waldegrave, who accounted for, I think, sixteen of these events, was a little crabbed-tempered horse, as narrow as a knife, and apparently not half big enough to gallop over a country, carrying anything like weight. His habits were very amusing, and one of his fixed ideas was that he would never be induced to "turn on the steam" in his three-mile training gallops till we reached the final bend for home; from that point to the finish—which he knew as well as I did—I had to do all I knew to hold him. In the early part of the journey, however, you might hit him, spur him, kick him if you liked, but never a jot did he alter from the easy canter he was in. Another of his peculiarities was that, in running, unless it was "his day," no power on earth would induce him to jump the first fence; and when he "turned it up" there, and commenced a stately walk back to the paddock, it was best to let him go without fighting the point out. I never met the man that could stop him.

Few men there are who went racing much during the past decade, that do not remember old Breach of Promise, who came out as lame as a cat, and hobbled down to the post like a bear on hot bricks every time he ran, and yet the number of steeplechases he won was surprising. Robert I'Anson, to my mind the finest professional cross-country rider I ever saw, used generally to ride him in his races. The famous jockey did not look much like riding at racing weights last time I saw him, on which occasion he was officiating as starter at Redcar races. Blessed with a fine frame, and no longer obliged to reduce himself to ride, you look at him and wonder how any man so big could ever have donned silk; yet not only was he most successful in his calling, but, considering the amount of riding that he did, his allowance of falls was a remarkably small one. He had a wonderful escape when, in riding old Scarrington, at Croydon, he, feeling the horse swaying about beneath him, threw himself off, only a few seconds before the poor old slave came crashing to the ground, stone dead. On Sir George Chetwynd's Lord Clive, he had a nasty spill in a hurdle race at Brighton, and was carried into the stand considerably more dead than alive. Still, on the whole, I think he would agree with me that he has been lucky in public, and what was probably his worst fall, occurred on the schooling ground.

Taking into consideration all the chances of steeplechase riding, it is really surprising how little serious harm is done, year after year. I confess that the views I held at twenty (*i.e.,* that steeplechase riding was about on a par, as regards danger, with travelling along in a goat-chaise) have been modified. A horse falling at a fence, and lying on top of me for some time, induced a distinct and immediate alteration of opinion, on that subject. Still, I think it is not so dangerous as it looks, especially if only old hands are riding. It is from the youth, whose chief anxiety it is, to know whether Tottie and Lottie are looking at him from the stand, and who is really riding excitedly and in a funk at one and the same time, that the element of danger comes. Should you, when going in front, have a bit of ill-luck and come down, be sure that it is this gentleman who will land on top of you. If, in coming over a fence, you suddenly feel a shock which half knocks you out of the saddle, causes you to lose a stirrup-iron, and makes your horse stagger and pitch on his nose, be satisfied that it is the same hopeful being who has collided with you. If kind fate ordains that he should get the worst of the collision, and turn over, mentally present an address of congratulation to yourself and fellow-riders on the happy event, for you will do the rest of the journey in comparative safety.

Of handsome steeplechase horses—and they run in all shapes, veritably—Congress always struck me as one of the best. He was a very unlucky horse in not taking the highest of cross-country honours, as he most assuredly deserved to do. Chandos, again, was a splendid specimen of the English thoroughbred, but it always occurred to me that hurdle-racing was more in his line, than getting over a country, despite his starting favourite for the Liverpool, won by Regal. He used to gallop with his head tucked into his chest in a way that suggested his not looking where he was going, and that mostly means an unsafe conveyance. As a hurdle-jumper, however, he was *facile princeps*.

Another of the handsome division was The Scot, a son of Blair Athol, who never showed much form on the flat. He, however, developed into a jumper of the highest class, and won the Great International Steeplechase at Sandown, and the Great Metropolitan at Croydon in 1881, carrying big weights. H.R.H. the Prince of Wales subsequently bought him, and, trained by J. Jones, of Epsom, who also donned the purple jacket, scarlet sleeves, and black cap in the race, he started first favourite for the Liverpool in 1884, but unluckily came down, when going well.

The late Mr. Studd's Despatch was as near a certainty at his fences as it was possible to get, in spite of his being an awful "star-gazer." What a lot of good horses there were running, about this horse's time! Disturbance, the winner of the Liverpool in 1873; Ryshworth, owned by Mr. Henry Chaplin, whose connections thought defeat impossible, and who was beaten for speed at the finish of that race, just the point where it was confidently anticipated he would shine; Snowstorm; Scarrington, whose death has been before alluded to, and who should have won in '72; The Lamb, who once performed the feat of jumping over no less than four prostrate horses and riders at one fence; old Scots Grey, one of the grandest jumpers that ever ran, and who, if my memory does not deceive me, kept on winning until he was over fourteen years of age; Marin; Footman; Schiedam, whom, I believe, Mr. J. M. Richardson considers the best he ever rode; Chimney Sweep, who fairly revelled in jumping, and did not know how to make a mistake; Silvermere, a very useful sort, in spite of being awfully " dicky " in front; Master Mowbray; Phryne, always invincible at Cheltenham; Royalist, on those rare occasions when he condescended to keep in the course, instead of bolting into the adjoining parish; Crawler; Primrose; and last, but not least, Mr. Arthur Yates's Harvester, winner of several good chases.

I never saw The Colonel—twice a winner of this coveted prize—but have heard that he was " as good-looking as he was good." He had " h. b." written after his name, as had Captain Machell's Hesper; though the latter never soared above hurdle-topping, he was a grandly-built one, and could carry lumps of weight at his own game. The same remark applies to Lowlander, who, with Hampton, was found far too valuable for the "sticks," and taken back again to the "legitimate" sport. Seeing the sprinter, Lollipop, win his races always caused me to think what a wonderful chaser he should have made, and had the Duke of Hamilton cared to turn the attention of this horse and Wild Tommy to cross-country work, they would have been a pair "bad to beat" over any course. It will be remembered what a remarkable fight Wild Tommy made of it, in Petrarch's St. Leger. Vigorously ridden by Custance, he reached the winner's girths, and then his neck, but could get no farther, and Lord Clifden's son just got home, "all out." Wild Tommy, Lowlander, and Lollipop were, perhaps, three of the most powerful horses that have been seen on the turf for years—16 stone would not have troubled either of them to carry to hounds.

For the generality of horses, I do think our weights are a bit too heavy. In the same way that the raising of the weights on the flat, say to a 6st., instead of, as now, a 5st. 7lbs. minimum—would be an unmixed blessing, so do I think that at least 7lbs. might be taken off steeplechasing weights, making the minimum here, 9st. 7lbs. You may own a remarkably smart horse, who is put up in the handicap scale so much, that, although he might stand a fair chance of giving the weight away to the rest, yet is not big and powerful enough to carry 13st. or 13st. 7lbs. three or four miles across country, and then, as in many cases, to race up a hill with it, to the finish. In my opinion, nothing is gained by putting these crushing weights on a horse, and surely, if it be right for an animal ever to carry them, then it would be for a comparatively short distance, on the flat, and not when he has to lift them over big jumps, at a time of the year when the ground is almost invariably in a heavy state, and under conditions which make the course two miles in length, at the very least.

Although instances are not wanting of unlikely-bred ones taking kindly to jumping, there is no doubt that it "runs in the blood" in most cases. All the Solons and the Uncas's, the Flash-in-the-Pans and The Lawyers, seem to have the gift, and in such a list we must not forget Xenophon and New Oswestry. Lothario has got some good chasers, and hunters to boot; and here and there—as with Industrious, winner of the big hurdle race at Croydon, Sweet Galingale, and The Scot—Blair Athol is represented between the flags in a favourable light. Still, partial as I am to him, I cannot put forward the latter sire as anything like so famous in this way as most of the others named. Roughly speaking, one may say that all the Irish horses jump, and probably for the very simple reason that they are taught their business earlier in life than our own.

With the abolition of the suburban racecourses, very much that was ruffianly and disgusting was swept away, though one cannot help a sigh of regret for Bromley's natural fences and running water, that had to be negotiated in real hunter-like style. It was on this course that one of the worst outrages ever committed took place, Charles Lawrence the steeplechase rider being the victim. I had the story from his own lips, and feel that no excuse is needed for giving it here. In this particular race, there were four starters, and whilst going round the far side, some miscreant hurled a brick, which struck him full in the face, felling him like an ox. " He might have saved himself the trouble," said Lawrence, to me, in his nice, quiet way; "I was on the worst horse of the four that started." Unhappily, the scoundrel has never been discovered, from that day to this. Had he been caught, and handed over to the tender mercies of the law, "with any luck, and Hawkins up," as they say, such an amount of retirement, at the expense of a paternal Government, would have been meted out to him, as would have satisfied a very glutton. Once " in," he would certainly have been converted into a "stayer," by the sport-loving judge!

Casse-Tête, Shifnal, Pathfinder, and Zoedone may all be accounted a bit lucky, in being returned winners of the Grand

National, and it would be an easy thing to name several others, of the same periods, who never enjoyed the distinction, but yet were infinitely more worthy of it: such, for instance, as Harvester, Scarrington, Schiedam, Scots Grey, Mohican, Cyrus, Too Good, Congress, and The Scot.

In Casse-Tête's year there was a regular chapter of accidents. About half the journey had been accomplished, when Primrose fell, and Schiedam was brought to grief by coming over on top of him. Mr. J. M. Richardson, who was on the latter, was unhurt, but of course the *contretemps* put his chance out, and soon after Mr. Arthur Yates had to pull Harvester up, as the horse cut his hind foot very severely, and Scarrington seemed to be walking in, when, to I'Anson's unspeakable disappointment, the old horse cut himself so badly at the last hurdles, that he could do little more than hobble past the post, and Casse-Tête finished practically alone.

Shifnal had nothing much but "crocks" to beat when he won, and his victory is chiefly pleasing for the fact that, by it, the name of Robert I'Anson was enrolled, as it thoroughly deserved to be, amongst the winning riders of the cross-country Blue Riband.

Pathfinder, again, in '75, was opposed by a poor field, and was certainly a long way the worst of "Mr. Thomas's" three winners. Not long after riding in this, his eighteenth Grand National, this gentleman, a most resolute man on a horse, got a horrible fall at Sandown, which affected his sight, and, of course, he was never seen in the saddle afterwards in public.

Zoedone, ridden by her owner, Count Kinsky, a good man over a country, plodded on and won in 1883, from the smallest field on record. The mare could stay for ever—at her own pace; but that is not, as a rule, good enough for Liverpool, and one wag suggested that she should be started overnight.

At her next essay, the following year, the mare blundered badly two or three times, and finally fell. It was pretty generally understood that some miscreant had got at her whilst she was in the Paddock, just before the race.

Of the brace of winners that Mr. J. M. Richardson so brilliantly rode, Reugny was not supposed to be nearly so good as Disturbance. It must have been hard work to get the former home at all; he was so done, that he went right through the final hurdles, never rising an inch, and very nearly landing on his head.

Many essays have been made, with varying success, to win big steeplechases with horses in the "hunter" class. Eurotas, invincible amongst the "certificated" division, proved only a splendid failure, when flying higher. Pathfinder and the Liverpool '86 hero, Old Joe, on the contrary, were fully equal to the occasion. No grander horse than The Sinner, by Barabbas, another hunter, has been seen on a racecourse for many a year, and had he been left in the Grand National of 1887, I do not think 11st. 10lbs. would have checked his extraordinary career. I think I am correct in saying that this horse was ridden to hounds by a lady before Mr. Craig had the good fortune to secure him and The Gloamin for 600 guineas. I wonder what would be his price now! The strange thing about him is, that he seems equally good whether he is carrying Mr. Thirlwell on the flat or across a country ; and as to weight, he is so big and powerful that it seems to make no difference to him at all. Withal, he is, I am told on high authority, as easy to ride as a pony. His race at Croydon, in March,

'87, wherein he met the crack hunter, St. Galmier, and conceding him weight, beat him with ease, was a real treat to witness. At the same time, Count Kinsky's horse is by no means to be under-rated, and he would undoubtedly have gone closer but for making a serious blunder at the Farmhouse open ditch, and nearly coming down. This obstacle is really a very formidable one, and if the Croydon Executive could manage to soften Mr. Bevill's heart, on this point, they would have a course, leaving absolutely nothing to be desired. Mr. George Lambton rode St. Galmier, and although unsuccessful on him, decidedly had all the best of the meeting in other respects, winning the Grand International Hurdle on his great fine mare Bellona, and on the following day taking the Great Metropolitan Steeplechase on Sir W. Throckmorton's Phantom. He rode a brilliant finish on each occasion, especially in the hurdle race, when Bellona appeared to have a bit the worst of it with Silver Sea, until close home.

Prominent amongst cross-country horsemen who have ceased practice recently occur the names of Captain Arthur Smith (better known as "Doggy" Smith), Mr. J. M. Richardson, the Hon. Greville Nugent ("Mr. St. James"), Robert I'Anson, Lord Melgund ("Mr. Rolly"), Mr. Garrett Moore, Mr. Arthur Yates, "Mr. Thomas," and one may include Mr. Arthur Coventry, now that he has confined his attention to flat racing.

Of those now riding, Mr. E. P. Wilson, Hon. George Lambton, Mr. Brockton, Mr. D. Thirlwell, James Adams, Jewitt, C. Lawrence, Captains Owen and Lee Barber, the whole family of Beasleys, Mr. W. H. Moore, Skelton, Mr. C. I. Cunningham, Sensier, Barker, and "Gus" Lowe must be named as artists of the highest stamp.

CHAPTER VII.

CONDITIONING AND SCHOOLING.

SINCE the "summer at grass" system of resting hunters has almost been numbered with the things of the past, the question of conditioning does not enter so largely into the scheme of horse management as it did. Coming up from grass, meant, in most cases, a weak-looking neck, coupled with an inflated carcase to begin work upon: endless physicking, and a very gently graduated system of dietary, and months, or, at the least, many weeks, before daring to give a gallop of any kind. All that is altered now, and men at last recognize the paramount importance of never letting a horse get *out* of condition. A roomy loose-box, well ventilated and clean, with, perhaps, a couple of hours' run in the day, in a paddock, and about two feeds of corn, is the way to summer hunters; they are not torn to pieces with the flies, and allowed to get weak from want of corn, neither do they knock their feet to pieces on the turf, at a time of year when it is mostly as hard as adamant. Then when you take them up there is something to work upon; they are fat, clean on their legs, and all that is needful is to get their wind clear, whereas if they had been depending chiefly upon grass for their sustenance, you would have weakened, and, poor animals, have to *fatten,* as well as train.

The first thing to be done when a horse

is brought up is to get his coat off, if it is at all a heavy one; nothing is more weakening than for him to have a coat like a blanket, to do his work in, nothing freshens him up so much as clipping it off. Then a mild dose of physic, such as a four-drachm aloes ball, having, of course, previously prepared him for its reception by a short course of bran mashes, &c., and when quite over its effects, you can go to work on him in earnest. Two hours a day walking exercise for the first week will be enough, and then some slow, steady canters, gradually increasing in length, should be added to the walking exercise. Never let a horse get to his fullest speed, on any account, whilst either conditioning for hunting, or in training for steeplechasing. Horses always run best when a bit above themselves; the leading trainers of the day have long since recognized this, and the consequence is that far fewer of the dejected, hunted-to-death-looking wretches that used to be seen in the saddling paddocks of our racecourses, are visible now. In short, the Chifney school theories have been relegated to the "forgotten limbo of the past," and humanity and common sense, joining hand-in-hand, have swept away much that was harmful in the training stable, as they have practically smashed up the blood-letting quackery that our unhappy forefathers groaned under. Half-a-dozen good rousing gallops for the concluding week of your conditioning, and your horse is fit to go.

As to the time occupied in getting a horse fit, much, of course, must depend on the individual temperament of the animal. If he be of the light-fleshed sort, half the work needful for the gross feeder will be sufficient for him. Again, a horse that sweats very freely will usually " come to hand " much quicker than he of slower actioned skin. Then, also, it depends a great deal upon the condition you find him in to start with, and also upon his peculiar constitution. No hard and fast rule as to time could possibly be laid down, but, roughly speaking, from six weeks to two months ought to be long enough to get the generality of horses fit to go with hounds.

In schooling horses for jumping, whether you want them for hunting or steeple-chasing, no amount of time or patience can be too much for the business. The smaller the obstacle the better chance you have of getting him over it, at first. I have found that riding a horse over a farm, walking him through gaps in hedges, leaping little ditches, &c., is valuable by way of introduction, and after that a small obstacle made up of sharp, prickly gorse, and not exceeding three feet in height, will induce him—after, perhaps, once blundering through it—to rise nicely at it, as he will discover that his legs are not proof against prickles; if, however, he persists in blundering again, have a stiff rail run through it within a few inches of the top—when he has "rapped his knuckles" on this, he will probably find it worth his while to do it properly. If he won't have it in any other way, get off and lead him over; most horses will let you do this, and follow over almost anything.

After the gorse has been properly surmounted, the pupil will probably raise no very strong objection to a flight of sheep hurdles, and when these obstacles have been got over, something in the shape of timber may be thought of. When this period of the training arrives, most of the riders remember important engagements elsewhere!

Truth to tell, this form of entertainment is more exhilarating than peaceful! Well do I remember, in the days of my "giddy youth," being put up on a wretch, with the heart of a mouse, who had never been induced to jump a straw up to that moment. I had a scheme, a colossal scheme for making her jump a low rail, bushed up with furze. I made a bet I would get her over; the trainer thereupon indulged in the remark of "Didn't I wish I might get it?" or something to that effect, and then I commenced operations. Taking her right back to the other end of the field, I started at a hand gallop, and gradually pressed her till we were going as hard as she could lay legs to the ground. Then I pulled her round the corner of a park paling, that had hidden the jump from view, and she was almost on it before she saw it at all. The moment her eye rested on the obstacle, she began to "curl," and shutting up like a telescope, every stride, she made a frantic effort to stop herself, but two yards away from it I let the spurs in, and giving her "one, two," with the whip, she kneed the rail, smashing it to atoms, got half round, and then fell head over heels, bringing down a young fruit tree, the made obstacle with it, and my astonished self, at one fell swoop! The bet we made is in abeyance to this day, I maintaining that I "got over it," and my opponent that I "fell into it." I don't know who is right, but I humbly confess that if I *did* win that bet, it was not in the way I contemplated, at the time of making it!

Mr. William Day, in his excellent book, "The Racehorse in Training," strongly disapproves of the system of clipping, although he advances no particular reason for his dislike. Now, half the horses used for hunting, and a great many employed at the steeplechasing game, would be fearfully handicapped if their coats were left on. I have ridden several who would fairly stop with you, after galloping a couple of miles with hounds, enveloped in the long hair that comes in the winter season; and no less an authority than "Stonehenge" distinctly approves of removing the coat. Probably, however, Mr. Day was only alluding to flat-race horses, and in this particular I would not presume to offer an opinion, although I once owned a three-year-old Rosicrucian filly, carrying such a coat as would have been, to say the least of it, a very powerful argument in favour of the clipping machine. Personally I venture to go so far as to say that it acts as a powerful tonic, and will frequently enable a horse to throw off a slight cough or cold by its invigorating action. In the same chapter, Mr. Day quotes Buffon in support of his statement that "horses like a medium climate, bordering on cold rather than heat," and here I am quite of his opinion, instances too numerous to mention occurring to the mind of animals who never seem well except in the cold weather.

The system of sweating has very much gone out of late, but a steady three or four mile gallop, with the clothing on, will do no harm, provided it is not too often repeated: once a fortnight will be found quite sufficient, and great care should be exercised in rubbing down, and drying afterwards, to avoid the risk of a chill, as far as may be.

No better schooling than that obtainable with a pack of harriers, can be given to a beginner across country. The pace is slow as a rule, there is the gentle stimulus of hounds running to give zest to the work, and deprive it of the suspicion, always hanging about the pupil's mind, that he is being taught a lesson, and believing, as I do, that horses like hounds as much as men like them, it is only natural that they should, for their own satisfaction, try to surmount all obstacles that come in the way, whilst following them. "This," says Whyte-Melville, "is why the hunting-field is such a good school for leaping. Horses of every kind are prompted, by some unaccountable impulse, to follow a pack of hounds, and the beginner finds himself voluntarily performing feats of activity and daring, in accordance with the will of his rider, which no coercion from the latter would induce him to attempt. Flushed with success, and, if fortunate enough to escape a fall, confident in his lately-discovered powers, he finds a new pleasure in their exercise, and, most precious of qualities in a hunter, grows "fond of jumping."

There is one thing about which no doubt

whatever can be entertained: that confidence on the part of the rider will inspire confidence on the part of the ridden. A short time back, I was forcibly reminded of this at Kempton Park Steeplechases, on seeing the redoubtable "Gus" Lowe bringing the mare, by Ethus out of Candia, right along, in front of everything, and slashing over each obstacle, including those unholy open ditches, as though he had half-a-dozen spare necks in his pocket for self and horse. This mare, be it remembered, had never been over a country before, her previous efforts having been confined to hurdle racing. She won easily at the finish. Now, a man like that would do more to "make" a horse, in an hour, than a good many would do, in a week. In fact, the least bit of indecision is ruinous to an animal's nerve, when he is learning to jump. Not that I mean by this that a horse should be "butchered" at his schooling; that process is equally wrong; patience does not mean timidity, any more than butchering means pluck. Indeed, the last-named style of riding is very often adopted in order to hide the fact that the man is a member of that well-known regiment, the 1st Royal Hard Funkers. What a man Tom Cannon would make for the game, with his delicate hands, easy seat, and perfect patience! The Hampshire horseman, however, holds the opinion that married men, with families, have no business with steeplechasing and all its works, and I think he is about right. I am not aware whether the master of Danebury ever does any of the schooling *in propriâ personâ,* but he certainly turns out some admirable jumpers from his establishment. These used to be steered by Mr. Arthur Coventry, until that prince of gentlemen jockeys gave up cross-country riding.

An amusing thing it is to see a whole string of weedy wretches, cast-offs from the flat, ridden by large-headed and small-bodied boys, turn up at covert side in order to "qualify" for hunt races. Lashing out in all directions, and with "training stable" written palpably on their snaffle bits, saddle-cloths, and bandaged forelegs, they certainly look like anything *but* hunting. The crafty way, too, in which their riders watch the M.F.H., from whom they have to get their certificates, until he happens to be looking, and then rush their steeds, more often through, than over, a 2ft. fence, is very edifying. "What the devil do you want breaking down men's fences for?" yelled a much-harassed master of foxhounds, in my hearing, once. "Here you, boy, you can have your certificate and take yourself off out of my sight at once, and be d—d to you!"

I believe of course in power, thighs, quarters, muscle, &c., for jumping essentials, but, above all, do I believe in confidence on the horse's part; without this, all the other qualifications go for nought. Once establish thorough confidence in your pupil's mind, and you need not fear but that success is close at hand.

One more allusion to "The Racehorse in Training" I must make, before concluding these few remarks. In the chapter entitled "Jockeys," Mr. Day makes some admirable comments on the system of light-weight boy riders, and calls especial attention to the ignorance and incompetence existing, to so large an extent, amongst them. He is right, with a vengeance! Speaking generally, you might as well put up so many Marmoset monkeys to ride. The veteran trainer points out how grossly over-paid they are by winning owners, &c., giving *douceurs*, out of all proportion to the services rendered, and remarks that such a method of procedure is one eminently calculated to lead them, and does, as a fact, lead a large number of them, to ultimate ruin, besides being a great injustice to those owners who, from principle, or because they cannot afford it, refuse to follow suit. I have reproduced the substance of his observations, for the purpose of comparing the position and pay of these manikins, with those of the hardworking steeplechase rider, and the schooler of steeplechasers—men who, very often exiles from the flat for no other reason than that of increasing weight, daily risk life and limb on racecourse and training ground, and get comparatively little for it. If owners, instead of pampering ignorant, and for the most part bumptious, little boys, turning their heads with cigars and champagne, and giving them the wherewithal to surround themselves with a pack of yellow-haired "ladies," would reward older men, whose necks are constantly risked both in public and in private, in a more substantial fashion, it would be better for all concerned, and I would certainly extend these remarks so as to include a flat-race rider who had kept his master's secrets, or had had much wasting for any particular race, or ridden in the trial, or, in short, shown himself a faithful servant, win or lose. The dangers of the schooling ground are considerable, and deserve to be well requited. It was in teaching the gigantic Thunder (who afterwards made a very successful performer over the sticks) that poor Sam Daniels lost his life, and Robert I'Anson, the hero of a hundred victories between the flags, got his worst fall on the training ground. I believe Mr. Arthur Yates, Mr. Lambton, and Captain Fisher could also relate some personal experiences concerning injuries and broken bones, got in the same way.

I fancy that it is by no means so common a practice as it ought to be to have the spring bars of the saddle left open, so that if the foot gets fast in the stirrup iron, you, at least, have one extra chance of escape from dragging. All my life I have been in the habit of riding thus; but not long ago, a new hand adjusting the leathers, one hunting day, shut the spring bars up, and, as ill luck would have it, I got a rattling fall. My horse fell over a quickset, and pitched on the bank of a deep ditch, into which he rolled, my right foot firmly wedged in the iron. Three times did he struggle up and fall back again, missing me at each attempt. Now, it is ten to one that had those spring bars been open, my leather would have slipped comfortably out, and I should have been free. A short time since, I picked up a well-known master of hounds, after a bad fall, in which he would assuredly have been dragged, but for his stirrup leather parting company with the saddle, as the horse rose and galloped on. There are many kinds of patent safety stirrup invented, but though in pretty general use amongst ladies, men do not seem to take to them, somehow, and as far as I know I never saw one in use, except with the fairer part of creation. I have examined every invention of the kind, and though I have never seen them put to the proof in "actual warfare," several of them, doubtless, will answer their purpose. Some, however, are so manifestly ridiculous, that no practical horseman would give them a second thought. One of these latter articles, consisting of one stirrup inside another—there are several made that way however—would no doubt answer admirably, if you could make an arrangement with the Fates that, when you came off, you should be allowed to describe an exact semi-circle, ending well in front of your horse; but deviate an inch from that line, and this particular stirrup would, I venture to say, hang you up, much more securely than the old-fashioned iron! The best I ever saw, is one in which the whole inner iron turns over when pressure is applied, and, without any springs, opens naturally and lets out the foot. I don't know whose invention it is, nor the maker's name—if I did I would gladly give both, and take the risk of my reader's suspicions as to its being a puff! From its very simplicity I believe failure to be impossible, and it has as neat an appearance as the ordinary stirrup.

To give a horse two or three falls over timber, purposely, is, I think, a very doubtful expedient for making a jumper of him;

but when we find such "past masters" as Thomas Assheton Smith advocating, and Dick Christian condemning the practice, who shall take upon himself to decide the knotty point? The latter authority says: "They talk about a young horse wanting falls. If a young horse gets a very bad fall it frightens him. A couple of falls with low fences are well enough—*but not if you hurt him.*" Now, perhaps the real strength of this expression of opinion lies in the words I have italicized. You must by no means hurt, or frighten, your horse. If you do, you destroy his confidence, and possibly ruin him for ever for learning the business. From my own small experience, I am still in "open mind," having tried the experiment with four horses, and failed with two of them; neither would ever look at a fence again. Many horses, after getting a severe fall, lose heart and courage, and become determined refusers. Whenever this happens to a horse who has been a good jumper he should be thrown up at once, for at least a month. By the end of that time, he will probably have got his pluck up again, even if he has not forgotten his tumble, for horses' memories are inconveniently long, on all points!

Captain Machell, at Kennett, near Newmarket, and Mr. Arthur Yates, at Bishop's Sutton, Alresford, have jumping schools for the early teaching of beginners. Stiff posts and rails, about ten feet high, enclose a track, in which, on a graduated scale, all sorts of obstacles are fixed, from the small hedge to the uncompromising wall, which will not bear playing with. Into this, the learner is turned loose, and driven over the jumps by men behind him with whips. This is an excellent plan for many reasons, one of which is that it involves no risk to human life or limb, and another that the horse gets into the way of taking his leaps in the manner most comfortable to himself, and, therefore, in the safest way. Of course these schools are for steeplechase horses solely, but, were they obtainable, there would be no better way of teaching a young hunter his business.

The great difference between the education of the hunter and the steeplechase horse is that the former may be taught in the way that allows him to take his own time on landing over his fences, whilst the latter's chance of success in his calling would be absolutely *nil*, unless he can "get away" as quick as a rabbit after his leaps. Dick Christian said, "I never rode a steeplechaser yet but I steadied my horse on to his hind legs, twenty yards from his fence, and I was always over, and away again before the rushers." True wisdom this, but I am afraid that nowadays there are some steeplechase jockeys who would beat anyone following this advice, by their reckless habit of "chancing" the last fence in a race. If they don't come down, they gain an immense advantage, in the run home, over the men whose horses really make a jump of it. Then the veteran rider goes on to say that a horse should land over his jumps on his hind legs, *i.e.*, that his hind legs should touch ground before the fore legs. I hope, in the face of so great an authority, that I shall not be deemed presumptuous if I venture to think that such a thing is a physical impossibility. I do believe that the hind legs should follow up the fore legs so closely as to make their respective landing almost simultaneous; but I would ask all men who are in the habit of constantly riding jumpers whether they do not always distinctly feel the fore legs touch first?

Very often a horse is pronounced fit to run in a steeplechase, long before his jumping education has been completed.

The animal who has managed to brush over a few flights of hurdles, and win his race, is considered quite fit to tackle a steeplechase course, after scrambling once over the jumps on the schooling ground, probably not half the size of the obstacles he will have to encounter in public. No first-class trainer would be guilty of such culpable recklessness, of course, but, unfortunately, there are a large number of men, who, not having the piloting to do themselves, care little whether their charges jump or fall and break their riders' necks. Education, to be of any use, should be thorough in every detail, and whether for profit, as in steeplechasing, or for pleasure, with hounds, experience plainly tells us we should aim at getting a "performer." One would be safe in saying that over ninety per cent. of the steeplechase horses of recent times, have spent their whole lives before entering upon their career as jumpers, in flat race training stables, and have done nothing else. There are some curious instances, though, of animals having come from unlikely spots, and of having even done "general utility business" before running over a country. Mr. Studd picked up his Grand National winner, Salamander, out of a wretched Irish hovel, with a coat on him like a polar bear. Baron Finôt, greatest of French steeplechasing owners, once drove a horse in his brougham to the course, took him out of harness, had him saddled and a jockey put up, and he won his race in a canter. Conservative—one of the most wonderful jumpers I ever saw, and, by the same token, the ugliest, commonest-looking beast in the world—was bought out of a drove, and, being a black, put to the business of "corpse collecting," as an irreverent friend of mine expressed it; but after making a bolt with the hearse one day, was turned over to a butcher, and driven, for some time, in his cart. Whilst in this humble vocation, he was seen and bought by a gentleman, who rode him with staghounds, and then put him into training. I myself saw him run second in a good field at Sevenoaks steeplechases, after twice bolting with so accomplished a horseman as Captain Fisher on his back. So fond of jumping was he, that I have seen him, when turned out in a field, jump backwards and forwards over a quickset, big enough to stop most horses, for the pure fun of the thing!

The Liberator was popularly supposed to have been drawing bricks before he ran in his last Liverpool (though I do not vouch for the truth of this); and a horse I knew well, was doing ordinary carting work on a farm, when he was not wanted for schooling a string of half-a-dozen steeplechase horses over their jumps.

CHAPTER VIII.

THE SHOW-YARD IN RELATION TO HUNTERS.

"IF a horse will jump in a show-yard, he'll jump anywhere" is an expression we often hear used, and doubtless there is a good deal of truth in it. But will he jump so big? "Not by a long way" is the answer that experience unhesitatingly makes, nor can anything be plainer than the reason why. All conditions are favourable for the effort in the show-yard—the horse is fresh, has only just had exercise enough to stretch his muscles, the ground where he takes off is light and sound, the jump itself free from traps of any kind, and the rider (usually a light-weight) is therefore enabled to send him at it freely, and with perfect confidence. Now, in hunting, the horse is called upon to perform under very different circumstances—the ground is generally deeper, the weight he carries heavier, and perhaps he has been half-blown by a hard gallop, over ridge and furrow, before being asked to do a big thing in the way of jumping. There are, it is true, a few phenomenal leaps on record "in the open," such, for instance, as Chandler's extraordinary effort on the Warwick steeplechase course, when he cleared thirty-nine feet; Mr. Tom Smith's horse, who, after one refusal, jumped the wall of Elcot Park, in the Craven country, which said wall was a solid six feet, two inches in height! Sir Charles Knightley, on Benvolio, cleared thirty-one feet, over a fence and brook. Jem Mason succeeded in topping a five-foot-six gate, made of stiff, new timber, in a steeplechase, and I am afraid to say the exact height of the Marden deer park rails over which Gregory, the jockey, was carried by a runaway youngster he was training. I know the place well, and "Gregory's leap" is certainly one of the most formidable obstacles I ever saw. Then there is Emblem's leap at Liverpool of 33ft. Still, after all the examples of big things done with hounds, steeplechasing, &c., they pale before the show-yard record, and, as I have endeavoured to point out, it is only natural they should. The high jump at the Agricultural Hall at Islington is, to my mind, an unfair thing to ask horses to try, and those that do get over it, do not, and cannot, jump it in anything like business fashion : they cannot *see* over it, to go no farther. Every time I have seen a horse jump this obstacle—I will not pledge myself to the exact height, but believe it to be something about six feet six—he has sprung into the air in a half-maddened manner, and with no very definite idea as to where he will land. I do not think such feats as these are a true test of a horse's merits, nor do they prove anything about him, one way or another. Were I going to purchase, from the performances in the Ring, I would much rather take the animal that topped the gate neatly, and then showed cleverness in getting in and out of the "double," than the one that succeeds, by a wild and unnatural effort, in clearing the high jump. On the whole, the show-yard hardly seems to be a reliable testing-place for hunters. How many are there, I wonder, who—real "flyers" in the hunting field—simply decline to look at their fences when brought out in a tan-covered arena and surrounded by a noisy crowd? Plenty won't jump in cold blood *at all*, and anywhere, let alone in a circumscribed space, with the crowd thrown in. One chestnut mare I knew of, on the contrary, would jump almost anything you liked to put her at, so long as she did not see hounds —once let her catch sight of them, and good-bye to comfort and the chance of getting her over fences. She went fairly mad, and would—after making frantic efforts to dislodge her rider—put her head down and rush like a bull at the first obstacle, then whip round and bolt in the opposite direction, thereby affording any rider in search of a little healthy excitement about as much as would last the average man for a month! Another, belonging to a friend of mine, who hunts down in the happy Vale of Aylesbury, used to serve him in much the same way, her performances culminating in the breaking of her own jaw, and nearly drowning her rider, by falling into a brook on top of him, and my unfortunate friend thought himself a lucky man to escape with a broken leg.

I have said enough to show that, in my humble estimation, not too much reliance should be placed in show-yard performances when choosing hunters; the conditions under which they act are so different that this is hardly to be wondered at, when carefully thought over. "Men talk of blood, make and shape, muscles, quarters, backs, &c.," said an old sportsman once, "but I say, give me a horse with brains. He has to take care of the bigger fool of the two, and think for both." Now, some jumpers have a wonderful supply of brains —and some, I am inclined to think, have them not at all. As an example of the latter, what brains does the average "rusher" possess, I wonder? The perverse beast, who *will* have everything at forty miles an hour pace, whether there is a chalk pit beyond or not? or the brute who goes boldly to his jump, and then, half "turning it up," drops, faint-heartedly, into the middle of it? But look on the other side of the picture, and there you see the full force of the old man's remark—"Give me brains." See the extraordinary cleverness, which guides so many of the best hunters, season after season, and gets them over, and out of, so many difficulties. There are few greater treats, to a true sportsman, than to watch an old hunter's performances, over every variety of fence, and especially to see the way in which he will extricate himself from any trouble that may—I had almost said must—befall him in the ordinary course of his career.

There were some extraordinary jumpers at the Aquarium, some time ago. I understand that the equine "boss" of the show was an Australian, and, ridden by Miss Nellie Reed, he was in the habit of clearing a gate 5ft. 8in. high, daily, whilst another, picked up for £30 at Tattersall's, did almost as well. I wonder if Miss Reed would have cared to take her mount at a five-foot gate, out with hounds, especially if the ground was at all poached by cattle? The highest recorded jump in the show yard is, I believe, that of the American horse, Hempstead, who successfully negotiated an obstacle 6ft. 8in. in height, at the New York Horse Show, in the autumn of '86. Australian horses seem to share with Irish-bred ones, a natural gift for jumping, and though the "walers" are not the easiest things in the world to ride over fences, their prowess is undeniable. A horse called Leo, an American, belonging to Mr. "Freddy" Gebhardt, and standing seventeen hands high, did 6ft. 6in., before coming over here to compete at the Agricultural Hall, in the weight-carrying class, in June, '86. At that Show, the most extraordinary jumper, to my mind, was an evil-tempered iron grey, admirably ridden, by a man whose name I do not know. This horse, after standing on his hind legs, and fighting the air, suddenly dropped and almost flew at the high jump, launched himself madly into the air, and, somehow or other, got over in safety; one or two more accomplished the feat, but all, as I before said, with the air of not knowing where they were going to land.

There have been some enormous leaps recorded out of the show yard, but doubt has been thrown on a good many. For instance, many men say that the measurement of Chandler's historical effort at Warwick—39 feet—is unreliable, and that Emblem's 33 feet in running for the Grand National at Liverpool—when she is said to have taken off, 12 feet in front of the obstacle, and cleared three or four feet beyond the brook—is "stretched," but there can be no question that a tremendous lot of ground was covered by the latter on that occasion, though it may not have been quite what is stated; for my own part, I believe both measurements were accurate. There is no doubt as to Mr. Tom Smith's leap over the park wall already alluded to, a stupendous and desperate performance. To my mind, fifteen feet of water is quite big enough for any horse to attempt, and there are remarkably few " certainties " in the country at that. A good twenty feet would have to be covered "to do the thing well," and that is a lot of space to get over anywhere, but on paper.

At some of the horse shows, in this country, an open field is available for the jumping trials, and, in such cases, a much more natural test of a horse's capabilities can be applied than in a covered-in and limited space, especially if the crowd can be, to any appreciable extent, got rid of.

In choosing hunters from the performers at such places, one is far less likely to go wrong in the open than on the ordinary tan track. Given one's choice, however, and there can be no doubt at all about the fact that more is learnt about a horse in a ten minutes' fast spin, over a good country, with hounds, than by any amount of trials in cold blood, wherever they take place.

One word upon the subject of the pivot swung jumps: are they an unmixed blessing, or not? It is true that they give way when rapped hard, but I have seen a horse turned over, very nastily, by them, for all that. I incline to the opinion that a made jump, lightly resting against supports that will give way on being struck, is the safer of the two. In fact, it is very difficult to see how an accident could happen, when such obstacles as these are used. The pivot-fence swings its lower part very awkwardly in the way of a jumping horse, and is somewhat apt, on occasions, to catch his hind legs whilst in the air.

What an interesting study it is to stroll through the Agricultural Hall, when the Horse Show is on, and watch the wondrous and fearsome "get-up" of 'Arry. A splendid type of this *genus* presented itself to my marvelling gaze one day when I was up there. His hat was tip-tilted over his left eye, and a rakish-looking covert coat enveloped the upper half of his manly form (by the way, why *will* counter-jumper youths persist in wearing these comfortable riding garments, when never do they, by any chance, get on a horse?). Tight, leggy trousers, of *prononcé* stripe, and a twopenny white tie, with a large horse-shoe pin, completed his costume. Evidently well satisfied that his attire was calculated to impose on the credulous, and make people believe in his profound know-

ledge of horseflesh (which, by his remarks, I should say, was confined to that retailed on little sticks for the benefit of the feline race), he fixed his eyes upon a spare, cadaverous-looking man, dressed in a brown loose wrapper, dark trousers, and a none too new top hat, who was looking fixedly at a little blood chestnut, then going into the ring. Quoth 'Arry to his pal—
" 'E looks as if 'e knew a lot about 'orses, *I* don't think," with great demonstrations of disdain. The spare man's face was a study; he had overheard the remark, and had to turn away to hide a grim smile. He was a well-known gentleman rider, and probably the finest horseman, either on the flat or across country, in the whole of the Southern part of England! Poor little 'Arry! Well was it for thee that thou wast unaware of what an elaborate ass thou wast making of thyself at that moment!

CHAPTER IX.

CROSSING A COUNTRY.

BEFORE attempting this " labour of love," every man, who values his own comfort and safety, should run a careful eye over his horse's appliances. " Not one groom in a hundred knows how to bridle a horse properly," says the author of " Riding Recollections," and certainly an astonishing amount of ignorance *does* exist upon this very simple matter. The throat-lash is almost invariably too tight, and so are the saddle girths. Another common fault, also, is not having the head-stall long enough to let the bit lie comfortably in your horse's mouth without "crumpling up the corners of his lips," to quote the same writer again. Most grooms seem to think that in girthing a horse up the correct thing is to pull and drag until the animal can hardly breathe, and they themselves get black in the face, from their wholly unnecessary exertions. To fix the curb-chain properly also seems quite beyond them, their one idea being to make it as tight as possible. All these matters require the careful attention of riders themselves, and a few moments spent in this way will not, by any means, be wasted. For most horses, the best possible bit is the short hunting curb and snaffle. The proportion of horses tender-mouthed enough to ride to hounds in a plain snaffle is comparatively small. For a hard puller, nothing beats a sharply-twisted snaffle, with a double rein and martingale. As to the gag, I never saw the hard puller who cared twopence about it. It is a hideous and ridiculous contrivance, and the most useless of the many devices invented for stopping this sort of horse. A band or net, across the nose, is much more effectual.

How amusing it is to hear men telling their friends at covert side, in tones for everyone to hear, that they are "not going to ride to-day; they have only come out to look on!" Well, who on earth wants them to ride? If they are in a funk, by all means let them stay away, and not make a pretence of hunting when their nerve has left them. It is surely no discredit to a man to lose his nerve, but it is a very ridiculous thing trying to conceal the fact, under this flimsiest of disguises.

Now, I venture to think that, in cross-country riding, the power of the legs is, or ought to be, paramount. Here it is that the fair sex are placed at such a terrible disadvantage; it is true they can, by means of the pommel, get a certain grip of the saddle and security of seat, but they have no method of communicating what they are thinking about to their horses—a very serious drawback to equitation. A man should do everything by the pressure of the thighs and calves, and especially should he tell his horse by that means the exact moment at which he ought to take off at an awkward place, or, indeed, at any place, or else *let him alone altogether!* Half the secret of success lies in this—take off a stride too soon, and see what it adds to the size of the leap. Do so a stride too late, and probably you will not see, but *feel* what the effect of so doing is, with stiff timber! In order to get the full effect out of this leg power, both the hands ought to be on the horse's withers, a rein in each. So riding, it will be far easier to steer him at his jumps, and far harder for him to get the chance of refusing them.

Assheton Smith laid down three canons for crossing a country, that we may all well lay to heart. The first was that "there is no place you can't get over, with a fall;" the second, "no man can be called a good rider till he knows how to fall," and as the writer averaged over sixty falls a season, he ought to be a judge; and the third, "throw your heart over, and your horse is sure to follow." This last maxim deserves special commendation. You must make up your own mind about the matter, or surely you can't expect your horse to do so. Put your eye on a place, and say to yourself, "I'm going to have it *there*," then let him swing along freely at it, tell him with your legs *when* to take off, and trust him for the rest. Assheton Smith certainly practised what he preached; notably so when, going to covert one morning, he rode the young one he was on, three times at a stiff 4ft. rail, each attempt resulting in a fall; the fourth time he cleared it successfully! It takes a man tolerably *hard* for this style of schooling, I fancy! *Head* is an all important thing in the field; without discretion, what is the use of pluck and resolution? And the converse, of course, equally applies; a man may have the judgment of a Solon and the wisdom of the snake, but *minus* courage, and where is he? And echo answers, where? Certainly not at the finish of a run—unless he came round by the road! As to the former class, old Jim Hills, the huntsman of the Bicester, used to say of the Oxford undergrads, who rode at or over his hounds, in addition to anything else that came in their way, " Bless you, sir, they fears nothing, *'cause they knows nothing!"*

Now, men of this stamp are bound to come to grief, seriously, sooner or later, and the sooner the better for the safety of the rest of the field. See the finished horseman, as he goes down to a fence, on excellent terms with his mount, neither pulling at him nor letting him out-pace himself, but gently restraining him, so that his head is nicely "in hand," and he can feel him well, and know exactly what he is doing. A big open ditch, and strong-staked and bound fence beyond, form the obstacle. The rider sees that his horse must be roused, and encouraged to jump his biggest; he catches him well by the head and sends him resolutely at it. The horse, knowing by the touch (this is not a good way of expressing what I mean, but it is the best I can think of at the moment) of his pilot that he is *intended* to jump, gallops up to it, straight as a die, takes off, in obedience to the pressure of his rider's legs, at the right moment, and clears it all in good style. He is immediately followed down to the leap by the man who is all pluck and no head, and what happens? He has been sending his horse along a bit too freely, and in consequence thereof he is a little blown. Directly our friend catches sight of the task before him, he says, " This is a big one! " and thereupon does he cram his hat on his head, and drive his horse as hard as he can at it. " When you see a man going a hundred miles an hour at his fences, depend upon it that man funks," said Assheton Smith. Quite true, as a general rule, but not so in this instance ; this man feels no touch of funk, but having no discretion and head, pace is his one idea of tiding over the more formidable obstacles he meets with. But to resume. Our example's horse, hurried off his legs, and with his head sticking awkwardly up in the air, takes off too soon, strikes the top of the fence very hard, and turns a complete somersault into the next field. Both these men had courage, but only one had head with it.

The exception only proves the rule, and in reference to the "hundred miles an hour" system, I have known it to be of considerable value in the case of a determined refuser. In fact, one wretch that I was condemned to ride (for my sins, I suppose) a whole season, could only be induced to jump anything when sent at it so fast that she had to go either "in or over!"

It has always been, more or less, a matter of surprise to me, to notice how small a margin a clever hunter will allow himself, either in landing on the farther side of a brook—when sometimes it looks to you, who are riding, as if only his forelegs could possibly reach the bank and the hind ones must go in—or at a high jump, when you will often either hear the smallest perceptible rattle of the hoofs on the top bar of a gate, for instance, or find, by careful watching, that he has cleared it with barely an inch to spare. A horse's discrimination, and power of measurement with the eye, are remarkably correct, and even when so beaten that he feels rather disposed to "chance" his fences, he yet, in most cases, makes a very accurate shot at what is required, as a minimum of exertion, for clearing them. *A propos* of chancing fences, the one fall that a man has no excuse for is that which is caused by a horse being so blown that he comes down. This is frequently the worst kind of "downer," too, as a beaten horse falls "all of a heap," and perfectly helpless; if he is on top of you, then it is usually a bad business. The rider may always know when his horse has had enough of it; his laboured breathing and heaving sides, the "flop" of the ears and constant changing of his leg, tell the pitiful tale all too eloquently, and the man who goes on after such warnings, does so at his peril. One might add, that the man who goes on after such warnings ought to be kicked! But this is detail.

Perhaps men who tell you that the only way to ride to hounds is to "take your own line, and keep it," don't quite realize the force of what they are talking about. In most countries you have to follow in single file over many of the fences, which perhaps only boast one practical place apiece. Again, you are probably not on the fastest horse in the field, and, given that single file, or something like it, is the order of the day, you can't either take the lead, or keep it. Neither is it desirable so to do, and many horses won't jump, unless with a lead. In addition to this, it would not be pleasant to see men continually racing to be in front, nor is it a sportsmanlike thing to do. "Circumstances alter cases," and when one gets into the Vale of Aylesbury, for instance, it is easy enough to ride one's own line, as most of the fences are as jumpable in one place as another. Of course the same observation applies equally to many other countries, such as most parts of Leicestershire, Northamptonshire, Gloucestershire, the Blackmoor Vale, *cum multis aliis,* too numerous to mention.

Lots of men shirk timber, and prefer anything in the shape of a natural obstacle, even with the chance of an uncertainty beyond. Assuming that the former is only of reasonable height, I think it, with most horses, is infinitely preferable; it is clean, you know exactly how much you have got to do, and nine animals out of ten like it better than a thing they cannot see through. By saying this, I don't mean to recommend anything in the shape of Jem Mason's five-foot-six gate, be it understood!

Why do many men still stick to the old-fashioned practice of throwing up the right hand in the air, as they go over a fence? I never could understand the "why" of it, as the Yankees say, any more than Mr. F. G. Hobson's curious habit of putting his hand on the cantle of the saddle, under the same circumstances. Both seem to unnecessarily weaken the rider's powers, and you want *both* your hands, not only before rising at, but also in landing over, your fence, to collect, and assist your horse into his stride again.

Another thing is, that throwing your whip-hand into the air must alter the position and balance of your body at the critical moment when your horse is "taking off;" nothing is more likely to cause a flounder, if not a fall. A man who rides at his fences with both hands, one on each rein, well down, has twice the power of the one who voluntarily sacrifices the use of one of those hands.

Some men seem to steal, or glide, imperceptibly over a country, as it were, and others to butcher across it. Naturally there is a great deal of difference in the animals ridden: some only want holding, some driving at their fences; still, so much depends on whether a man wants to "flourish," or whether he has simply the sportsman's desire to be with hounds.

Although it may not be either practicable or desirable, in many countries, to take a line of your own with hounds, it certainly is both practicable and desirable in steeplechasing. There the fences are as good in one place as another; there is no "uncertainty" to look out for on the other side, and if a man will persist in following exactly in another horse's track, naturally he must come to grief, should anything happen to his leader. It is not nice, either in hunting or steeplechasing, to have a man riding in your pocket, and no one fancies being danced on by a follower when he comes down. Constantly is this glaring fault committed on the racecourse, and even putting aside the question of danger, both to horse and man, it doubles the odds against your standing up to the finish, because, assuming that you, who are following, get safely over your fence, if your leader should peck and come down, over you must go with him, to a certainty.

In the few observations at the beginning of this chapter will be found one upon the subject of tight girths, and being anxious not to be misunderstood on this subject, I venture to recur to it again. Though I am no advocate for tight girths, believing that when moderately girthed, and a breastplate used, the horse is far more comfortable, and quite as safe, still I have in my mind too sad an incident to recommend that they should be left, in the least, *slack*. I daresay many of my readers will remember to what I refer. The accident happened in a steeplechase at Cambridge several years ago. As the first and second horses actually passed the winning-post, The Priest's saddle slipped round, and his rider broke his neck on the spot. Strangely enough, the man who was second to him told him of the condition of his girths at the starting-post, but, unhappily, the ill-fated man paid no heed to the advice given, to tighten them.

One of the most useful things possible, to teach a hunter—and the process of teaching him is extremely simple—is to follow you about. In case of a tumble, which necessitates your letting go the reins, your horse, instead of galloping off, and leaving you to cross a country, uncomfortably attired in boots and breeches, will remain standing still; should your foot hang up in the stirrup iron, you will find it even more valuable than in the former case. An officer of Artillery, himself a good man to hounds, first called my attention to this. He made all his horses follow him about, like so many dogs, simply by coaxing and caressing them, feeding them with sugar, &c. One morning, waiting for hounds to come up, he gave me a performance, with a hunter, in an Inn yard, where some twenty vehicles were standing. The gallant Major dodged in and out these things like a rabbit, but his horse was just as quick, and would not be denied. I was so impressed with the performance, that every horse I have had since then has undergone a short and always successful (they learn so quickly) training in the trick, and on three occasions since I have found it of the utmost value, in falls. My friend said that he always had a curious idea that some day, in action, the fact of his horse standing by him in the event of an upset, might be more than useful.

A separate chapter of the excuses made by a certain class of humbugs who follow hounds—when they don't run—would be amusing, but would take up too much space here. The man who, on approaching a big fence, invariably believes that he has "lost a shoe," the man who "would have had" something that he palpably shirked, had he "been on the bay, instead of the chestnut," and the man who has "only come to look on to-day, and not to ride, you know," are familiar characters to us all. They have an explanation for every piece of funking, and really delude themselves into the belief that people are as big fools as they could wish them to be, in order to swallow the rubbish that they talk. If a man is afraid, why on earth doesn't he say so, and stop at home?

A keen eye for a country is a gift we all underrate in youth, and naturally, for our motto then should be that of Assheton Smith—"to go into every field with the hounds," and in such case we do not require the knowledge that enables us to ride to points. But when the nerve has gone—wholly, or in part—when old age or ill-health have robbed us of the precious gift of going, then does this science enable us to see much that is pleasant, much that recalls for a few brief, happy moments, the more stirring scenes of a time when we were able to ride with the best and hardest of them. I speak with especial envy of this knowledge, as I have it not, in the remotest degree, myself. In fact, if I once lose sight of hounds, nothing but a lucky accident enables me to fall in with them again, and I invariably lose my way coming home from hunting, even in the country I have been constantly riding over for nearly fifteen years!

I dearly like to see an old man, past riding straight, struggle gallantly along through gates, gaps, and lanes, arriving in time to see the finish of a good run. One game old Post Captain I know, sees a great deal of the runs, in the Blackmoor Vale country, in this fashion, and I well remember that my own grandfather, when past going straight, was never so happy as when engaged in the same manner.

Should any man be doubtful in his mind as to the spirit in which to ride across country let him take a copy of the following lines with him, and refresh his memory by perusing them at covert side. Here they are, and Egerton Warburton, good man as he was at the game, never wrote truer words than these —

> Give me the man to whom nought comes amiss,
> One horse or another, that country or this,
> Who, through falls or bad starts, undauntedly still
> Rides up to the motto, *be with them I will !*

CHAPTER X.

LADIES IN THE FIELD.

NOTHING causes greater divergence of opinion than the advisability, or otherwise, of ladies riding to hounds. Now, there are riders and riders, amongst the fair sex, as amongst the inferior part of creation, and most hunting men have, at some period or other, suffered severely, by reason of the vagaries of those, no doubt, charming ladies who, for instance, look winningly at you just as you are putting a horse at a gate, and coolly ask you to stop and lift it off its hinges! And, again, at the hands of the equestrienne who comes out with her husband, or brother (who are never at hand when wanted), but without a servant, and who persistently drops her crop, or her handkerchief, and mutely appeals to you for the restoration of her missing property.

But the lady riders who suffer from an over-abundance of pluck, and corresponding lack of discretion, are they who, seriously speaking, cause the terrible heart sickness we all, alas! know too well. It is a most peculiar thing that they seem to have so little knowledge of when a horse has had enough of it, and so small an appreciation of the size of obstacles. In saying this I am, of course, not speaking of the very front rank of lady riders, but of the general mass. Some years back I remember being, with some ten or twelve other men, fairly stopped, after hounds had been running hard for a quarter of an hour, by an apparently unjumpable park paling. Whilst we were cursing our luck, and consulting hurriedly, as to the best way out of the trap, a lady, who had got a bad start, galloped up, with slack rein, breathless, and excited. Immediately she saw the situation, she turned, and, unhappily fixing her eyes upon me, said, " Oh, *would* someone give me a lead over!" Well, there was no help for it. I was, luckily, on a steeplechaser, and was too great a moral coward to refuse, so, hardening my heart, I caught him by the head and rammed him at it. There was an unholy rattling of hoofs, but we got over—with a scramble! Needless to remark that the beautiful cause of this exhilarating occupation never got her horse over at all, although she tried most pluckily, half a dozen times. Their pluck is in nearly all cases undeniable, but—they are *not* judicious.

Watch how the average woman rides at her fences. No attempt made at holding a horse together, always the slack rein, and often the whip accompaniment, whether it is wanted or not! Not pleasant this, for the pilot, assuming that she is riding to one—much the safer and wiser way, be it said. To assume the somewhat difficult post of "leading" a lady, a man should be *facile princeps* at the game himself, it is needless to say, as he has to be responsible for the safe conduct of two, instead of one, in getting over a country. He should also be gifted with the strongest possible nerve, and ride a horse pretty smart at getting away, on landing over his jumps, as ladies are apt to be a little too quick and close on their pilots, and especially if their horses pull hard, or are of an excitable nature. I have, more than once, looked over my shoulder and seen the fore-feet of my charge's animal apparently over my horse's back. In a big jumping country some years ago, I, in a weak moment, offered, on the morrow, to pilot my then host's daughter. I did so—but "never again." I had to jump every fence, and then jump back again to persuade her to try it, although she was on a finished performer! After the first three minutes of the run, we saw hounds no more! But, with the average fair rider, it is only necessary that she should not follow you too closely, and that she should keep an eye on you, to watch for any signal to stop. This should be given by throwing the whip-hand up, in case of, for instance, a big drop, which you don't think safe for her to attempt. I piloted one excellent rider throughout a whole season, over a biggish country, and by her watchfulness for, and implicit obedience to, the signals, all but the most insignificant mishaps were avoided.

Whyte-Melville very properly says that "even if their souls disdain to follow a regular pilot, I would entreat them not to try 'cutting out the work,' as it is called, but rather to wait, and see one rider at least over a leap before they attempt it themselves." He goes on to say: "It is frightful to think of a woman landing in a pit, a water course, or even so deep a ditch as may cause the horse to roll over her, when she falls. With her less muscular frame, she is more easily injured than a man; with her finer organization, she cannot sustain injury so well. It turns one sick to think of her dainty head between a horse's hind-legs, or of those cruel pommels bruising her delicate ribs and bosom. It is at least twenty to one in our favour every time we fall, whereas with her the odds are all the other way, and it is almost twenty to one she must be hurt."

It is of the first importance that a lady's hunter should be perfectly broken, naturally temperate, and have plenty of brains. I once saw a lady's horse fall into a V-shaped ditch. The mare rocked to and fro, but judiciously let alone, she steadied herself, and with one big effort, and without the least appearance of excitement, she struggled out successfully. It was head alone, here, that saved a "crushing match."

Personally, I have always failed to understand how on earth any grip can be obtained on a side-saddle. Ladies, I know, say that it affords a much safer seat than our own, on account of the second pommel enabling them to press the left knee upwards from the stirrup. I have tried cantering on a side-saddle—it was uncomfortable, very. I started trotting—it was agony! Nothing would induce me to ride over even a flight of hurdles on one!

Again, they are deprived of that invaluable "touch" of a horse which their—I was about to say "lords and masters," but will substitute "slaves and servants," have. However, the fact remains that they *can* and *do* ride on these saddles, in a way that we cannot beat on our own, and so no good purpose can be gained by arguing the matter. The safety stirrup, before alluded to, should always be used, and an *active* servant (the fat old family coachman is *not* the man), or friend, told off to attend them during the day. These things being granted, there surely can be no valid reason advanced against ladies in the hunting field.

CHAPTER XI.

STEEPLECHASE COURSES AND POINT-TO-POINT RACES.

THERE has been a great cry at the downward course of steeplechasing of late, and undoubtedly there has been, if not a decline, certainly a "depression," in the sport, in recent years. Local meetings, in especial, have suffered, and chiefly because the farmers, and men who own *bonâ-fide* hunters, feel that they have no chance against the man with a thing out of a racing stable, which has hardly ever seen hounds in its life. People indolently say, "What a pity," and then add, "It's rather sharp practice, you know;" but as to taking any vigorous steps to remedy the abuse, that is the very last thing they think of. I wish the words "sharp practice" had never been invented; performances such as these should be called by their right name—obtaining money under false pretences. The owners of such horses well know that little local meetings are not got up, nor the money subscribed for their benefit. Nevertheless, a pack of unscrupulous ruffians are always ready to sneak unfair advantages, and spoil the sport. Lots of men who have their two or three hunters, animals that have honestly done their work with hounds all the season, would run them for the sport's sake, independently of any monetary value to the stake, and the farmer, who owns a good jumper and fairly fast one, would often be willing to try conclusions with those of a similar stamp, in public; but they argue, "What is the use? Something in the shape of a racehorse is sure to be entered, and mine, of course, stands no chance against that." This accounts, in great measure, for the paucity of entries and consequent slackness of the interest taken in meetings. Be the conditions what they may, some clever rogue seems always able to drive the proverbial coach and six through them. The question is, whether the evil cannot be attacked from a totally new quarter. Suppose these gentry, having carefully railed their "certainty" down to the station nearest the scene of action, found themselves confronted, not by the monotony of "galloping" fences, with the two regulation open ditches, but by a course comprising a bank with ditch on each side, a post and rails of uncompromising strength, and a "double," which would be certainly calculated to perplex the ordinary racecourse chaser. If to this could be conveniently added four or five stiff, natural thorn fences and some open running water, unguarded in any way, it is not improbable that the "certainty" would return to the railway station without having been stripped!

In some local steeplechases the conditions are that the competitors shall be half-bred horses, but considering that The Colonel, twice a winner of the Grand National, and Pathfinder, who also won, had "h. b." put after their names, it will be seen that the remedy lies not here.

There is another evil in the present state of the law regarding the qualification of riders. Several men who have had "Mr." prefixed to their name, and ride as gentlemen, are notoriously paid for their services. Others are either trainers or grooms, and in one case a grocer's assistant was actually qualified! At one meeting, I myself saw a groom ride, whilst a friend of mine, a member of the English Bar, had to stand down because he was not qualified! Such ridiculous nonsense can but do harm to the sport, and the restriction of "farmers or their sons to ride" is still more tiresome, as many "farmers or their sons"—if they happen to have any—don't feel disposed to risk their necks, or, more often still, have no knowledge of *how* to ride in a steeplechase—a very different thing to going with hounds—and, if this is the case, they must not put up anyone else, so their horse does not run. A very useful alteration in the law would be to admit, without further qualification, all members of the leading professions, as is done in the case of the Army now, such as Barristers, Doctors—very useful men to have about a steeplechase course, by the way—and Clerg—! (I nearly said it!) I know two or three men myself who dare not qualify, for fear of damaging their professional prospects, and yet who would be a valuable acquisition to the best interests of the sport.

Of late years there has been a partial revival of the good old-fashioned "point-to-point" steeplechases. The great—almost the only—objection to them, is that very little can be seen of the contest unless you ride with them. The conditions appended, which are those commonly used, will best show the nature of these chases:—

POINT-TO-POINT STEEPLECHASE.

Private Sweepstake of   sovs. P.P. for horses that have been regularly hunted with the   Hounds. Owners up. Catch weights [or to carry   stone.] Over about   miles of fair hunting country, from point to point, to be named by Messrs.   . Riders must not ride for more than 100 yards at one time on a road or lane, nor open a gate. Entries to be sent to the Hon. Sec. on or before the   day of   .

Sometimes it is advantageous to omit the words "owners up."

There are frequently two prizes, one for horses carrying over 13 stone, and the other for those carrying anything less. Sometimes both classes are started together; sometimes separate events are made of the contests. In any case, it is real good sport, and a very genuine test of a hunter's capacity. A useful condition in these races is that none of the competitors shall have ever been in a training stable. This sometimes works rather a hardship upon the man who has been regularly riding an old chaser, and perhaps it would be better to make it a little narrower—say, that no horse should be allowed to compete that has been in a training stable within the twelve months immediately preceding the start.

The movable feast of the Grand National Hunt Meeting—for the G.N.H. Steeplechase is run on a different course each year—generally brings out some promising performers. The race is for *bonâ-fide* hunters that have never won, either on the flat or across country, a race value 20 sovs., and that have never started for a handicap, steeplechase, or hurdle race: weight for age. The value of the event is about 300 sovs., and the entrance is only 3 sovs., the sole liability for non-starters. Amongst the winners in past years are: Schiedam—probably the best horse that ever started for the race—piloted most ably by Mr. J. M. Richardson; The Duke of Hamilton's Bear, who never did much afterwards, on account of a "pain in his temper;" and Mr. Vyner's Bellringer, who, at his best, was a good horse; as was also Lucellum, another winner of this prize.

Not content with giving the unprecedented sum of £10,000 to the Eclipse Stakes, a mile and a quarter race, the Sandown executive, ever marching with—

perhaps even a little in advance of—the times, has offered a princely sum for a mammoth Hunters' Steeplechase, to be run in 1888. This should, and probably will, attract such a field to the post as has rarely, if ever, been seen before. The experiment of giving large sums to hurdle races has been a great success, so far as attracting large fields is concerned—and to Croydon belongs the honour of leading the van—no less a sum than £1,200 being added for one of these events, as far back as 1875, when I saw little Industrious, a son of Blair Athol, romp in, through a sea of mud, with W. Daniels on his back. The winner started at an outside price, and the colours of all the jockeys were so plastered with mud that he was not recognized at first, and many thought it was his stable companion, a hot favourite, who had won.

Red-coat steeplechases are pretty often

introduced into the programme of hunt meetings, and, in my humble estimation, might with advantage be eliminated, as it is perfectly impossible, in running, to distinguish the competitors, and a description of such races must needs be of the vaguest kind. As sensible would it be to start a field for an ordinary flat race, with all the jockeys attired in "the Grafton scarlet!" I think, myself, that it would be an unquestionable advantage for the riders to sport ordinary colours, even in Point-to-Point races.

In concluding these brief remarks, it might be respectfully sugested to the G.N.H. Committee that the open ditches should not be made compulsory on natural courses; in such places they are nothing more or less than an unnecessary nuisance.

CHAPTER XII.

THE MUDBURY HUNT DINNER.

AT the conclusion of last season, it was determined that the members of this distinguished Hunt should give a dinner to the farmers of the surrounding neighbourhood, and accordingly, on the appointed evening—the invitations having all been accepted to a man!—the little Inn yard at Mudbury was the scene of great commotion, caused by the continuous arrival of all sorts of odd vehicles conveying the guests to the scene of action. There was a strong dash of the market-gardening element, by the way, amongst our farmers, and most of them were "little men" as to their holdings, having probably started as labourers on allotments; consequently there was no foolish over-refinement about these sturdy sons of toil, and a large proportion turned up in corduroys. The guests were received by our Master, Lord Swellboro', whose sole drawback is that he has only two ideas in his head—hunting and racing. He knows nothing else—seeks to know nothing else; the rest of his life is, metaphorically speaking, coma.

Slight deafness, and an almost irresistible impulse to use bad language on all occasions, complete his more notable characteristics. In this last little weakness, however, he does restrain himself, this evening. Punctually to the moment, amid a great slamming of doors and scuttling of feet outside, something in waiter's attire (I afterwards found out it was the helper in the stables) announced that "dinner was served." A regular scramble for places then ensued, interspersed with, "Will you sit here, Mr. Phatted?" "This is my place, I tell 'e," "I don't know who you are, sir, but—" "Waiter! how can I sit on a chair without a back to it?" "That's my bread, sir," &c., &c., but at length people all shook down into their places, somehow or other, and the feeding duly proceeded. There was a little dissatisfaction felt when, upon a dish of sweetbreads being offered to him, Mr. Jorker took it out of the servant's hand and emptied the whole lot on his own plate, nor did Mr. Muttonface increase his popularity by helping himself to a whole pheasant, one of the brace on the dish before him, and declining to carve the other "not to please no one; he come there ter eat, not ter carve." However, these little matters being adjusted, and Mr. Jorker having topped up with a little cold game pie, after he had finished all the sweets he could lay his hands on, Lord Swellboro' rose, and as soon as the clatter of knife-handles on the table had partially subsided, he began, " Gentlemen, amongst the manifold duties of an M.F.H., there is, perhaps, none more pleasant, none of a more distinctly gratifying character, than that of bidding a hearty welcome to this board, to the farmers and landowners of the surrounding district " (applause). "To the young farmers of this neighbourhood who come out with us, I say ' Continue long to let us see your ug— well-known faces at Covert Side.' To the old foo— farmers, who do not don a racing jacket—I mean a hunting coat, I say, ' You are always a familiar sight '"—(here My Lord got rather mixed in his mind), "' and a pleasant one'"—(hear, hear)—"'on our land.'" (No one in the room understanding what he meant, the speaker himself least of all, this last remark was received in a mystified silence.) "I venture to say that a pack of foxhounds benefits the farmer as much as it gives pleasure to the follower of the chase." ("Yah!" ejaculated Mr. Pigbody, disgustedly. "Sh—sh," said the members of the Hunt, frowning at him.) "Just as the owner of racehorses benefits the trainer, so do we benefit you farmers. We say, 'Grow your corn'" ("For yew to come gallopin' over it, I s'pose," *sotto voce* from Jorker), "'and breed your horses, and we will buy them of you.'" ("At a price," audibly remarks a man who has tried the experiment, and found it "wanting.") "Our national sports should always be encouraged, and to you, the farmers of England, we look for that encouragement" (hear,

P

hear). "Racing" ("For rogues," growls one), "steeplechasing" ("For maniacs," grunts another), "and foxhunting," are things which—er—are ever calculated to 'cheer but not inebriate,' as the immortal Nelson observed at the Battle of Waterloo," concluded our Master, with a rhetorical flourish, in which facts were not "in it" with a very misty imagination! Everybody applauded at the finish of the speech—probably because it *was* the finish—and the noble lord resumed his seat and his cigar, only to rise again, momentarily, to propose the health of the farmers, which he had entirely forgotten in the course of his speech, although it was for that express purpose that it was delivered. He coupled the toast with the name of Mr. Pigbody, who, having filled himself a tumbler of green chartreuse, and taken a good pull at it first, was regularly rib-roasted on to his hind legs by his next-door neighbour. " My lordship and gentlemen all," he began, ("hic!") "wen my old ooman see your kind inwitation, she says, 'Tummas,' she says, 'if you 'as a chance o' speakin' at the dinner, don't forgit to remark that if you was them you should think it was more perliter to arst the missuses as well;' so I says I would, and now I've a-done it before I forgot all about it, so you'll please excuse me for a-mentionin' it, praps a little premmyture, as the French says. Gentlemen, the hobserwations as 'as fell from my lord is puffeckly true, and it does us all proud when the 'ounds come gallopin' all over the land, a-cuttin' up the wheat and playin' old —" Here the speaker was nudged violently by his next-door neighbour, and pulled himself up with a jerk. Resuming, after a further application of chartreuse, he said—"My lord says, 'Grow 'orses and breed corn.' Well, 'ed better try it hisself, and then tell us 'ow 'e likes to sell 'em for 35s. a quarter. Thirty-five shillins a quarter (hic!) is seveny shillins a 'alf, and two arves make 'ole. I means two seveny shillins makes (hic!) makes—" (aside to his neighbour, "Wha'stwiceseveny? Eh, whayousay? 'unnerdanforry?'") "unnerdanforry shillins for a 'orse, seven pund for a 'orse. Whasagoodathat? Think man breedorses forseven (hic!) puns? Iss p'rfeckliridicklus." And so saying, Mr. Pigbody stuck the lighted end of his cigar in his mouth, and glowered savagely upon everybody. Someone having surreptitiously removed his chair, his attempt at resuming his seat was hardly a success, and, as he explained next morning, the hearthrug, taking advantage of his back being turned to it, seemed to suddenly rise up and hit him. He disappeared from view, and no more was seen of him for the rest of the evening. During Mr. Pigbody's speech, Mr. Jorker had been pretty busily occupied filling one pocket with figs, seeing which, young Chaffaway quietly contrived to load up the other with olives, liquid preserved ginger, and two pairs of nutcrackers ; he also emptied the contents of the salt-cellar in, whilst the worthy farmer was looking the other way. Having completed these arrangements entirely to his own satisfaction, Mr. Chaffaway managed to induce the Hon. and Rev. Adolphus Whey—Lord Buttermilk's son—to change places with him, and so be in the pleasant position of receiving the full broadside of the irate victim's wrath, when the time of discovery should come. The health of the Master was then proposed by Mr. Whey, who, mildest of curates, had had an important episode in his life. He had been out with the hounds on one solitary occasion, whilst an undergrad. at Oxford. True, he didn't go far; for at the first obstacle, a hedge nearly two feet high, he fell off, and at once walked back home. Nevertheless, it was a thing to be fondly looked back to, fondly (and with a certain amount of prolixity) dwelt upon, and on the strength of the performance, Mr. Whey rather wished it to be understood, that, if not a hunting man exactly, it was entirely because he did not feel it consonant with his calling so to be, and not from any matter of choice. He began—" In rising to undertake so formidable and yet so pleasing a task as this, I feel that a more unworthy person might have been chosen—I mean that I am a more unworthy person than has been chosen—no, I mean—" (" Get away forrard! get on to him! get on to him!")—

"that is —" (here Mr. Whey gets hopelessly confused, and alternately smiles and blushes)—"when I rise to propose this toast, I feel that—er—in so rising to propose this toast, I am proposing a toast that you will all drink and see drunk with acclamation." ("Drunk with what?" inquires our slightly deaf Master.) "This toast is a toast which, above all toasts, should be *the* toast of the evening." (Here the constant reiteration of the word "toast" fairly put his audience on the rack—a veritable toast-rack.) "It is—our noble Master" (tremendous applause and jingling of glasses, lasting several minutes). "A master of hounds has no sinecure. What with his duties in the field—whipping-in and hunting the hounds, blowing the trumpet he carries at his saddle-bow, answering all inquiries made, and cutting off the brush when the fox is found, all his time is fully engaged; whilst, in the kennels, feeding such a number of dogs—for consider, gentlemen, the quantity of bones and cats' meat they must want—is indeed an onerous and responsible task. My own experience of the pleasures of the chase is, I regret to say, limited, though I must confess to a pang of envy when the spangled, —spotted beauties trot gaily through the streets of our borough. No words that I can use would suffice to describe the excellent qualities of your Master, and therefore I will say no more" (hear, hear), "but simply leave the toast in your hands." The whole company then rose, and shouting, "The Master!" drank to him, standing. In the enthusiasm of the moment Mr. Whey seized upon his neighbour's glass, and, with an airy bow to Lord Swellboro', was conveying it to his lips, when it was firmly caught, and wrested from him by the indignant rightful owner. Very much abashed, the unhappy gentleman, in great perturbation, hastily took up his finger-glass and drained it to the dregs, without discovering his mistake. They all then sang, " For he's a jolly good fellow ! " rather a superfluous number of times, and resumed their seats, as the Master vacated his. Having, at an earlier stage of the evening, exhausted his limited flow of oratory, he was rather understood than actually heard to say something about " Great kindness always received "—" quite unworthy "—" flattering terms "—" generous support "—" doing one's best "—" wild country "—" show sport "—" ably assisted "—" always continue "—" service of all " — " fox-hunting flourish " — " many thanks "—" kind way received toast," &c., &c. This over, Mr. Barney, the local doctor, a very ruddy-complexioned and obese young man, was called upon for a song. It was one of Mr. Barney's playful peculiarities that he must sing sentimental ditties of the tea-leaf and rose-water order, which he always spoke of as "little things." On this occasion he said he should be very happy to sing them a "little thing" called "Only a tiny wormlet." It was a very charming little ballad, with a plaintive high note at the end of each of the eight verses, but when he lyrically asked them to "lay him to rest on the lilies and dewdrops" one could not help the reflection as to what the lilies and dewdrops would look like after Mr. Barney's anything but ethereal fifteen stone had been put on top of them. A slightly hysterical recitation by an amiable elderly gentleman, with weak eyes and gold-rimmed spectacles, followed, and then an imitation of popular actors was given by the same individual. One felt thankful that he should have told us *whom* he was imitating, at the beginning of each sketch—it saves any misapprehension, as it were. It *was* a little awkward once, however, when on account of Lord Swellboro's deafness he did not catch the name given out, that of Mr. Henry Irving, and applauding loudly at the conclusion of the "imitation," said, "Capital, capital! Just like old Buckstone, isn't it?" This incident rather damped the performer's ardour, and, mercifully for us, shortened the series. When the time arrived for replying to the toast of "The Ladies," Mr. (he called himself Captain) Winker, of the 3rd Royal Blood and Carnage Volunteers, bounded to his feet in order to reply. Captain Winker's one o'ermastering desire in life was to be considered a "bold, bad man;" and if ever, my reader, you meet him and want to borrow a fiver, you have only to look knowingly at him, poke him in the ribs, and say that you know he is "the devil and all with the women," and success is yours. As a matter of fact, he is a most reputable member of society, and only " a sad dog " in the eyes of his maiden aunts. In appearance, he is short, round, and cultivates a small, ginger moustache, waxed at the ends, with an imperial, to give a martial effect to the *tout ensemble*. He is always intensely warlike, and, in keeping with this peculiarity, he has that of firing his sentences off at you, in a manner suggestive of small arms exploding. " When I found myself called upon" ("Nobody called upon him—he thrust himself forward," indignant aside from young Mr. Miggs, who wanted to respond himself) "to answer for the ladies—perhaps my enemies might say I had much to answer for in this way—" twirling up the right hand corner of his moustache, and waiting for somebody to laugh—nobody did, so he resumed—" I felt what a heavy responsibility was thrust upon me" ("Ass," wrathfully mutters Miggs). "We soldiers" (audible guffaw from Miggs), "we soldiers" he repeats, glaring, with glassy eye, at the offender, and speaking in louder, not to say aggressive, tones—" devils, perhaps, to our enemies, have still, somewhere beneath a rugged exterior, a spice of something gentler about us than we are generally credited with. Something soft" ("Like mashed turnips," interjects his pitiless foe, thereby creating an unmistakable snigger in his immediate neighbourhood) "there is beneath the surface of every warrior" ("Brains, probably," from Miggs), "which tames the fiercer portion of his nature, and conquers the ever-lurking desire to revel in scenes of carnage and bloodshed, and the desire to stand upon the tented field" ("After the fighting's over"). "And to what are we indebted for this influence?" ("Funk," growls Miggs). "To woman, all-vanquishing woman" (great applause). "What says the poet:

> 'Oh woman, in our hours of ease,
> Uncertain, coy, and—

("Apt to sneeze," chimes in his tormentor)

> '—hard to please.
> When pain and anguish wring the brow,

("They always make the greatest row!")

> 'A ministering angel, thou!'"

(deafening applause, especially from those of the guests who didn't in the least understand what he had been talking about). Very much gratified the little man went on: "Gentlemen, I will ask you to pardon me for invoking the Muse's aid once more in this most, to me, entrancing of all subjects.

The lines I allude to run something like this :—

> 'Oh woman ! watch the dying day,
> When night comes from the glen,
> And slumb'ring echoes seem to say—'"

("The old man's drunk again," roars the now infuriated Miggs, heedless of consequences). Oh what a scene there was ! it really looked at one time as though the crockery would fly. "Cad !"—" low ruffian !"—" my card, sir"—" ought to be shut up if you can't behave yourself"—" satisfaction"—" officers don't fight with blackguards, sir !"—" ginger-haired whippersnapper," &c., &c., until my Lord Swellboro' forcibly interfered, and succeeded, after a time, in pacifying the wouldn't-be combatants. Truth to tell, there was a great deal of froth about the affair, but very little, if any, desire for blood, on either side, and as Lord Swellboro's one fixed idea of reconciliations was to make both parties as drunk as they could conveniently get, he had them placed right and left of him at the head of the table, and having insisted upon their shaking hands, proceeded to fill both of them up, with all despatch, and finally had the satisfaction of seeing the pair of them into the same cab, a process replete with difficulty, as they each insisted on the other entering first, and finally, after wasting a quarter of an hour, decided to get in, at one and the same moment, arm-in-arm.

The rest of the company, having dutifully sung "God Save the Queen" in various keys—it was a sort of "go-as-you-please" contest, each performer making up his part as he went on—fell down the stairs and got home—at least those that were lucky did!

THE END.

www.ingramcontent.com/pod-product-compliance
Lightning Source LLC
Chambersburg PA
CBHW021828230426
43669CB00008B/903